A WAGER FOR ALE

THE STORY OF ARTHUR NAPPER AND THE ORIGINS OF THE STEAM TRACTION ENGINE MOVEMENT

CHRIS EDMONDS

Corinthian Publishers

By the same author:
A LITTLE AND OFTEN

An hilarious account of a life spent with the steam traction engine and fairground organ.

Dedication

At Arthur's special request, this book is dedicated to the memory of Tom Thatcher and Tommy Yeo.

Acknowledgments

I am very grateful to many people for all sorts of help and information. To Sally, my wife, for reading and correcting the manuscript and to Pam Appleby for typing it. To the Lady Helen Adeane and Mrs. Rose Lloyd (sisters of the late Miles Chetwynd-Stapylton) for supplying photographs. To Leslie Burberry, Alan Martin, Michael Lugg, Richard Willcox, Stephen Neville, Colin Hawkins, the Revd. Philip Wright, Alastair Dacre Lacy and to all those members of The Road Locomotive Society and The National Traction Engine Club who have shown a keen interest in this book. To my good friend Dr. Giles Romanes, Arthur's second challenger, for his entertaining and informative foreword. Perhaps most important of all, is my gratitude to Arthur Napper himself, for without his enthusiasm, patience and encouragement this story could never have been told.

Cover: Michael Rice

Foreword
by

Giles J. Romanes, M.A., F.R.C.S., D.O.M.S., Past President,
The Road Locomotive Society

The appearance of this book is not only timely, but also necessary and will be well received, so I am very glad to provide this foreword.

This story concerns a form of fun, fun to be had by people from all walks of life, some from country backgrounds, others who envied the lives of the travelling showmen and the equipment they used, people in the transport industry and not least the engineers and craftsmen in the iron trades. All of them enjoyed the fun of steam. Back in 1951 we did things with engines simply because it was fun and nobody who owned an engine then ever looked for approval, indeed, I was offered a psychiatric consultation by my chief, when I first drove my engine up to the hospital where I was a House Physician, "to see if I was quite right in the head"!

The five pound fine that I paid at Henley, which caused so much unpopularity to be showered on the authorities by the press, was a good bargain, because since then, no questions have been raised in this respect for any other engine owner. There might, however, have been just a lingering fear of prosecution, when I noticed that it had been planned that I was to be the last to leave the field, on the Twenty-first Anniversary Road Run from Nettlebed in 1975 and thus could run the maximum risk of getting involved in proceedings again!

I heartily agree that we should spread this fun to as many people as possible and it was for this reason that I alerted the press to the Nettlebed race. It was also the reason that I became member number two of The National Traction Engine Club and first Editor of its magazine, *Steaming*, which hitherto had been no more than an occasional news-sheet. I find it a continuing pleasure to see that the title that I concocted is still in use today.

Another side of the fun that we get from playing with engines is the number and variety of new friends that we make while so doing. I count myself very fortunate to have met Arthur Napper in particular, because I learnt from him skills in engine handling, threshing and agriculture, which would otherwise have gone unknown. In those days, he, too, was simply having fun with engines just for the sake of it, with never any thought of one day becoming famous.

You will all enjoy this book, which is a remarkably accurate history, easy to read and very amusing.

Giles Romanes
Portesham,
Dorset

July, 1985

Introduction

"Let us cherish our legends", wrote Harley Granville Baker, "for they are the spiritual side of facts". This book is about a man who is undoubtedly a legend in his own lifetime. He doesn't see himself in that light, it would be wrong if he did, and today he still views with mild surprise the enormity of the movement that grew out of what was, after all, just a wager for ale.

Today the traction engine movement gives pleasure to countless thousands every year and is now providing employment for some in a branch of engineering that, by rights, should have died out completely.

To many, it has become a way of life and in common with any great worthwhile movement, the original pioneers quite rightly become legendary. This, then, is the story of Arthur Napper, the Father of the Traction Engine Movement and, as Kipling once wrote, "t'was how it all began m'dears, t'was how it all began."

Chris Edmonds
Haddenham,
Buckinghamshire

January, 1985

Contents

Fowler number 20223, *Supreme*, under sentence of death in Hardwick's yard, Ewell, in 1949. Photograph: courtesy of Alastair Dacre Lacy.

Chapter One
To Sing the Song o' Steam

The modern traction engine rally is a phenomenon of our time. Every weekend throughout the summer, countless hordes of eager sightseers attend events from Cornwall to Scotland. Rallies are held in Ireland and have been seen more recently in Belgium and Holland. The craze for the return of steam power has blossomed in America, Canada, Australia and New Zealand. Apart from traction engine rallies, which may vary in size from, on one occasion, over one hundred engines in steam, to just two or three locals, no village fête or town carnival is really complete without a 'steamer' as its prize attraction.

Latterly, even the Lord Mayor's Show has boasted a pristine example of a Burrell showman's engine, or a Fowler ploughing engine dressed to kill. What was once a grimy workhorse of the period which ended abruptly with the Second World War, has been requested by Princess Anne to sound its whistle. Thereafter that particular engine bore the legend "presented before royalty".

It has been said that a steam engine is the boldest attempt by man to create a living thing and the comparison is not hard to make. First of all, no steam engine is simply switched on or off. It has to be woken by fire. No human is simply switched on or off either. There is a period of waking up at the start of a day and not many of us at our peak first thing in the morning. There is, too, a period of winding down at the end of the day, which applies to a steam engine just as much as it does to us.

A steam engine is not just filled up, it has to be fed periodically just as we do. If we don't eat and drink regularly, then we don't work well, neither does our friend the engine. If we eat or drink the wrong sort of victuals, or we eat or drink too much of either, we don't perform well either, or we fall sick. Here, too, the analogy holds true.

A modern diesel locomotive or agricultural tractor is constructed to work for mankind. A steam engine is never a slave, it is always a partner, it works *with* mankind. What I mean here is that if you drive a modern vehicle in a careless or slipshod manner you will, barring accidents, probably get away with it. Your care or lack of it will not be heeded or acknowledged one way or the other. A steam engine works with its driver, but never for him. The engine acknowledges careful firing and boiler practice by performing well and thus arriving at its destination or the completion of its work satisfactorily.

In terms of modern machine operators, there is really no such thing as a good or bad. They may be fast or slow, they may utilise the equipment beyond its designed speed or power, they may well ultimately smash it to pieces, but they will not tire it out. A steam engine overworked can get tired in the sense of a falling steam pressure, or overheated bearings, then, just like us again, it has to rest.

One of man's primeval urges is to keep warm. From the dawn of time, fire has saved man from freezing to death and it is the primeval urge that draws him to a fire. Man cannot exist without warmth, neither can a steam engine.

If then these conclusions make any sort of sense and there is after all this unique affinity 'twixt man and machine, then we need look no further for the reason for the vast crowds that annually return to traction engine rallies, or line railway embankments to glimpse a steam locomotive. Is it utter nonsense to claim that in our subconscious we see them as almost living things? If that is finally the heart of the matter, then we need look no further. Is that ultimately the fascination of steam?

Affinity with anything breeds affection and no other form of power has ever bred the love and loyalty that steam has. No car or aeroplane has ever been called *Bo Peep* or *Union of South Africa* and no-one has ever contemplated doing so. To name a diesel locomotive conjures up about as much ethos as naming a brick wall. Every schoolboy up to twenty years ago at least thought he knew what he wanted to do in life, nowadays they are not so sure. Perhaps with the current commercial opportunities opening up we may yet see the noble profession of engine driver return as a feasible lifestyle for the lucky few.

These thoughts may well be judged as just sentimental nonsense, especially by older readers who had to turn out in all weathers and for long hours, to coax work from leaking old engines long past their prime. Many drivers and owners cheered to see the back of steam and the dawning of modern technology, but many did not. How do we explain the sentiments of the engine driver who once expressed the opinion, that if he could have afforded to have done the job for nothing, he would have gone on doing it, or the steamroller driver who threatened to leave and take employment as a jobbing gardener, if his employer took the logical step of replacing the octogenarian steamer with its modern counterpart? What do we think of the steam ploughing contractor who stood and cried openly at the sale of his fleet of engines? Grown men aren't supposed to cry, but the demise of steam could make them.

By and large, the Second World War saw the end of steam on common roads. The Americans had designed heavy duty tractors, which flooded the English agricultural scene and rang the death knell for steam. The travelling showmen benefited in like manner from Army surplus lorries and four wheel drive tractor units, so 1958 saw the last of these one-time monarchs of the road. As is so well known, the Burrell, number 3849, belonging to the Essex firm of Presland's, saw the end of steam at the British fairground. The relatively humble streamroller soldiered on into the middle 'sixties, but only with drivers of the old school, who didn't mind getting up that extra hour early and took the maxim, cleanliness is next to godliness, very seriously, for they were proud of their work. They were, however, few and far between and the *new* maxim of, do as little as possible for as much as you can, swept all before it. King Diesel reigned supreme. It was, after all, cheaper and cleaner and more efficient and faster and above everything else it was modern. Keeping up with the modern Joneses was almost a religion, not only to farmers and showmen, but to the government as well. Steam was old-fashioned, so therefore Britain was old-fashioned and that, in the eyes of the world, would never do.

The very last traction engine of all was a Foster, built as late as 1944, number 14738. It was built for Messrs. Butterley and Co., but it must have been an anachronism even then and it only lasted a few months before being consigned to the scrap-heap. The steamroller was useful to a later date and Aveling Barford were still in business as late as 1948, constructing rollers to the Ruston design. Marshall's of Gainsborough, however, was still exporting boilers and parts, for assembly in India, until 1961/2. It has been learnt fairly recently, that in China, which was for so long a closed country, steamrollers of the traditional design and full size railway locomotives are still being built in Datong.

It could then be said that the building of the very last engine in this country, coincided with its virtual demise from common use. It is generally thought that the war years and the overwhelming need for scrap metal saw most engines destroyed. This was not the case, as the government was also aware that come the blockade, oil would be at a premium and if an engine was in working condition, then it could be used in agriculture. Not a few steamrollers were vital to the repair of runways and escaped the breaker's torch. Showman's engines were pressed into service to demolish inner city buildings and it is amazing to recall that during the Blitz in London, no less that thirty showman's engines were employed in the space of a few miles on this work; far more than one would ever see at one fairground!

It was when the War was over that engines became most vulnerable, as scrap prices rose quite sharply and many thousands of farmers, contractors and showmen availed themselves of this unexpected bonus and the chance to be rid of something that was by then quite useless. There were, however, those who somehow just could not bring themselves to do it. One can imagine the scene in yards up and down the country when the scrap-man came to call. "Got anything for me then?" he would ask. "Yes" the engine owner would reply, "you can take that old car body and those oil drums." "What about that old engine over there – you don't want that old thing do you?" "Well, I don't know," he would answer "perhaps when you come next time I might let it go."

Memories of journeys long ago might have flashed through his mind, scenes of threshing time, or ploughing time, or all the fun of the fair. The fact was, he had no need of that old engine, he couldn't use it, there was no point in doing it up because there was nowhere to exhibit it if he did, yet something intangible said he couldn't part with it. No other outmoded piece of equipment would ever have that amount of sway, especially when the whole country was feeling the pinch of wartime austerity.

Briefly during the War, the showman's engine had a stay of execution, being pressed into service demolishing bomb damaged buildings. Messrs. Smart's Fowler is seen using its wire rope on just such an exercise. They are probably gas cylinders, not bombs in the vehicle in front of the engine! Photograph: copyright Fox Photos, courtesy of Les Burberry.

As a rule that was about as far as it went. Just a mumbled apology to the scrap-man and a vague promise to destroy it at some time comfortably in the future. Engines just lay and rotted. Ivy weaved a leafy disguise as if to try and cover the plight of a once-noble animal. Small trees took root in tenders and smokebox doors banged idly in the wind. The cancer of corrosion ate inexorably into every sinew, until, almost as a last gesture of despair, the chimney would finally crumble and crash to the ground. It was a pathetic scene in yards all over the country and it seemed that nobody cared.

Was this to be the fate of the English traction engine? A single cylinder McLaren lying derelict in the New Forest in the 1950's. From the author's collection.

All was not totally lost, though, there was interest of a sort, perhaps only a glimmer, but it was there. It still tended to stop short at a refusal to finally destroy the engine, but there were one or two people who actually bought engines to stop this from happening. Luckily for us they tended to purchase anything they came across and some quite sizeable collections were built up, only in the main to be left to rot in their new homes, but at least it was a start. Perhaps the most famous of all was the late Christopher Lambert of Horsmonden in Kent. The collection that he built up was upwards of forty engines and, surprisingly, he periodically got steam up for a small select band of enthusiasts. The local populace was vaguely amused by this eccentricity and nicknamed the collection, Chris Lambert's Old Gentlemen. Such was his love of steam that upon his death in 1955, as a mark of respect, his coffin was carried past his favourite engine, an Aveling that he had re-purchased in order to save it, standing silently outside the church, out of steam with a wreath on the smokebox door. Not long before his death he met Arthur Napper and said to him "For years I've tried to revive interest in these old engines, but you did more in ten minutes than I managed in ten years."

Left: the late Christopher Lambert, who once said that Arthur's races did more in ten minutes to save the traction engine, than he himself had managed in ten years.

Bottom: just some of the collection of over fifty engines that Chris Lambert saved from the breaker's torch. Photographs: courtesy of The Road Locomotive Society.

As early as 1937, the Honourable Peter Hoseason of Dowdeswell Court near Cheltenham, was acquiring engines when he knew them to be threatened. The only survivor today is the Hornsby portable that is on exhibition in The Science Museum at Wroughton near Swindon. He managed to acquire what today would be considered some very rare and interesting engines.

He owned Burrell number 1007 of 1883, an eight n.h.p. single, which he had acquired from Chris Lambert and the Allchin traction, number 846, which he took off the hands of Messrs. Cambray & Co., a local firm in Cirencester. He also had an interesting little Mann tractor, which came from Messrs. Beckinsale and Co., of Corbridge, Oxon. Perhaps most interesting of all was the original B1 Tasker compound, number 1332, the prototype of that model. Finally he saved a little three ton Tasker tractor. He left Cirencester in 1939, presumably on war service and the engines became extremely vulnerable, in fact it is known that they were all cut up except one, as previously mentioned.

The late Chris Lambert's favourite engine: Aveling and Porter number 2384 of 1888. From the collection of Arthur Napper.

Other far-sighted individuals who tried actively to stem the demise of the traction engine were Messrs. Edwards of Swindon, who built up a collection of nigh on fifty engines at one time and the now famous George Cushing of Thursford in Norfolk saved the Thurston fleet of Burrell showman's engines, when they went under the hammer at a scrap-yard in Norwich in 1945.

Indeed the alarm bells were ringing and many people up and down the country were aware that unless something was done, the steam traction engine was in grave danger of extinction. Engines were indeed purchased, but their fate still hung very much in the balance, as a sudden rise in scrap prices could so easily have tipped the balance between sentimentality and the lure of hard cash.

In 1937 The Road Locomotive Society was founded. This was a learned society, dedicated to recording as much as possible about the various makes and makers, before it was all too late. It was a laudable project, but, like all other interested parties, they could only look back. They couldn't look forward, for there was nothing to look forward to, so restoration was pointless. What was needed was someone to create a reason for restoring an engine and, having restored it, a reason for using it. The man who was destined to do just that was Arthur Charles Napper.

The Aveling and Porter traction engine, which The Road Locomotive Society purchased from Naylor's of Maidstone in 1951 and which is now on show at The Science Museum, London. From Arthur Napper's collection.

The 1871 Aveling, restored by Messrs. Aveling and Barford and presented to The Science Museum by The Road Locomotive Society. Seen here arriving at the Museum. Photograph: courtesy of The Road Locomotive Society.

Chapter Two
Old Father Thames

Follow the river of that name due south from Oxford for about a dozen miles and you will come upon the village of Appleford. The river here is wide and slow running and it meanders across the fertile plain as if trying to make up its mind how to round the Berkshire Downs, which stand across its path to distant London and the sea.

The village is small and not overly pretty, unlike its neighbour, Sutton Courtenay. The market towns of Abingdon and Wallingford lie to the north and south respectively, for this is agricultural country. Being an alluvial plain, known as the Vale of the White Horse, the soil is good and productive.

The village itself has nothing to commend it architecturally and boasts nothing much older than Victorian, for it is really a railway village. Nearby, the town of Didcot sprang to life in the 1840's with the building of the Great Western Railway and tiny Appleford flourished when it found itself on the new main line to Oxford. Prior to that it was just a hamlet.

Its name denotes no more than a ford across the river and research shows that prior to the man who is the subject of this book, the village's most famous son was one John Faulkner, a racing jockey, who was perhaps even better known for his fathering of no less than thirty-two children. This feat seems not to have taxed his energy, as he died in 1933 at the incredible age of one hundred and five. It is perhaps a coincidence that where Faulkner made the village famous in the world of horse racing, there was to come a man from the same place, who was destined to make racing known almost the world over. Not racing horses made of flesh and blood, but a horse nonetheless; the iron horse.

The Napper family had been farmers in the Didcot area of Berkshire for over three hundred years. Grandfather Napper bought a farm at Didcot from Lady Wantage and upon purchase inherited the title, Lord of the Manor of Didcot. This would have endowed him with considerable privileges and prestige and, with other entitlements, he would probably have held the advowson of Didcot. He purchased more land, at East Hagbourne and Appleford. The farm at Appleford was cut in half by the building of the railway and it was the G.W.R. that was forced to erect Bridge Farm House in about 1840. The house in fact looks, at first sight, older, as it is based more on the Regency design and is not at all what one has come to expect of mid-Victorian railway architecture. It is very much a manor house.

Into this world on 9th February, 1920, was born Arthur Charles Napper, son of Frederick George and Elsie. He was born at Didcot and it would not have been surprising if Arthur had subsequently chosen a railway career, for the area effectively only offered one alternative: the railway or agriculture. The connections with the railway were there, for Arthur's maternal grandfather and uncle were both Great Western engine drivers, working from the Didcot depot. He has fond memories of both of them and of those days when one or other would take him on the footplate, giving him his first impressions of steam.

His uncle, Charlie Powell, used to tell Arthur many tales about life on the railway, at a time when the Great Western was at the height of its prosperity.

One such story concerned the time when he was working on the Lambourne branch line and rumour had it that a courting couple were in the habit of getting up to a bit of no good in a first class compartment. In the dark it was possible, from the footplate of the engine, to walk along the wide running boards of the coaches and observe the amorous proceedings. Charlie and his fireman used to take it in turns to go and have a look, but on the occasion in question, when Arthur's uncle returned to the footplate, he could see nothing but clouds of steam and boiling water. One of the gauge glasses had burst. It wasn't until, by holding his slop jacket in front of him, he had managed to get the taps turned off, that he discovered his fireman, as white as a sheet, crouching in a corner of the tender. The train had been driverless for more than three miles!

Arthur was one of three children. His two sisters were Joan and Maureen. Joan died tragically at the early age of forty-five and Maureen today lives in South Africa.

Schooldays for Arthur were spent at Didcot Upper School and in those days the régime was strict. Arthur was always more fond of the open air than the stuffy classroom and endless bookwork seemed tedious. He was, like so many of his generation, educated more by fear than any academic leanings and was far happier sitting up in the tender of the nearby steam threshing set, from where, on his return to school, he would again be severely scolded for having got his hands dirty. Once, when labouring over some essay or other, Arthur's patience with the ever-critical schoolmaster finally snapped: "This damned school is built on ploughed land that used to belong to my grandfather and I wish to hell it still was!"

Joseph Napper, Arthur's great uncle, operated this portable engine and tackle well before the turn of the century. From the collection of Arthur Napper.

Arthur grew up at Bridge Farm with the almost continuous music of the passing of Great Western locomotives, but it was the annual arrival of the steam threshing and ploughing sets that always interested him more.

The very first traction engine that Arthur can recall was a five horse Burrell and its driver, one Caleb Hitchman. "Now my little boy," he used to say to him, "if I let you sit here, don't you touch that glass tube or those pipes, because they're hot." Like any curious small child, it was, of course, the first thing that Arthur did!

In the early 'thirties there were four main threshing contractors in the Appleford area. W.J. Bosely of Harwell was employed to do the bulk of the work at Bridge Farm. He operated two sets, one of which was an interesting single cylinder Wallis and Steevens road locomotive, with one side of the belly tank cut away to allow for the driving belt. The other was a six n.h.p. Burrell compound. Charles Cauldwell operated a single speed Ruston and Proctor, which was originally designed for export and Thomas Thatcher and Sons had a fine single crank compound Burrell, named the *Pride of Berks*. Tom Thatcher and his two sons ran this firm and the name of the engine was not unfitting, as father Thatcher was a stickler for a clean engine. Such was Arthur's

The Napper family: Arthur's parents, two sisters and Arthur. From Arthur Napper's collection.

A youthful Arthur on horseback. From Arthur Napper's collection.

enthusiasm, that during his school days he would go out threshing with them and by the early age of eleven was learning boiler drill and the art of the thresherman.

His interest in steam was well known to his teachers and it was he who they looked for first when a tragedy occurred. Arthur recalls being summoned to the headmaster's study very urgently, to be confronted by a man obviously in a state of shock. "You're here, you're alive," stammered the headmaster. "Of course I am," replied Arthur, completely mystified.

Apparently a group of children had been playing hide-and-seek during the lunch break and one of them thought that he would never be discovered if he hid inside the threshing machine that was working near the school. The driver may have returned early from his break, ahead of the other men, perhaps to draw the fire up, but the small boy, one Jimmy Higgs, gave no warning of his presence inside the machine and when the driver opened the regulator, he was killed instantly.

The Police requested that the engine and machine be driven to Oxford so that a post-mortem could be carried out, but the driver was so overcome by what had happened that he flatly refused to take it.

Some six miles away in the market town of Wallingford was by far the largest firm of steam contractors in the area. This was Messrs. R.J. and H. Wilder, which is still trading today in modern agricultural implements, as John Wilder Ltd. Their fleet of engines covered all the

19

well-known makes and examples of Burrell, Marshall, Wallis and Steevens, Fowler and Aveling and Porter could be seen on threshing and other duties over a wide area of Berkshire and Oxfordshire. Perhaps they are best remembered for the four sets of Fowler steam ploughing equipment that they operated. These were lovely single cylinder engines with beautiful cast-iron bell chimneys. Working as they did every year at Bridge Farm, the sound of their throaty exhausts echoing across the wide fields was music to Arthur's ears. Wilder's subsequently built two engines, of which the boiler and tenders were theirs and other parts, such as wheels and gearing, came from Fowler's. One of this pair is, happily, still in existence.

Arthur, aged thirteen, oils up W.J. Bosely's compound Burrell in the summer of 1933. From Arthur Napper's collection.

By 1937, however, Arthur's father was beginning to complain about the high cost of contract threshing, so Arthur suggested that his father purchase a machine of his own. This he duly did and the machine was made by Garrett's of Leiston. There was then the problem of an engine to power it. On his own initiative, at the age of seventeen, Arthur went out and bought a seven n.h.p. Wantage single for the sum of forty pounds. He then hired the engine to his father for the princely sum in those days of one pound per week. Undoubtedly this was a commercial venture, but Arthur admits that it was a double delight to own an engine in his own right.

He got as much work for the old engine as he could, including numerous jobs hauling out trees for neighbouring farmers. One of the firms of local showmen was Sammy Williams', of Tadley, he being the father of Jimmy, who is so well known today at southern rallies. In those days Sam travelled with a set of Savage gallopers and organ, hauling them with a Fowler showman's engine called *Royal John*. The old Fowler only just made it to the annual Appleford Feast in 1938, as the tubes were leaking badly. Arthur wasted no time and lit a fire in the old Wantage. An hour or so later, he was crossing the railway bridge and on the way to the rescue. The front twisted brass cab support was removed from the Fowler and the driving belt put on the Wantage. With a few short, sharp barks from the chimney, the lights came up on the roundabout and Arthur was, for a couple of days at any rate, in show business!

Arthur's first engine. Both number and date are, unfortunately, unknown.
From the collection of Arthur Napper.

Tom Thatcher's Burrell single, *Pride of Berks*. From Arthur Napper's collection.

Tom Thatcher's colonial Ruston single being towed away for scrap, behind the Burrell, *Pride of Berks*. Tom Thatcher is standing on the left. From Arthur Napper's collection.

His great friends in the world of the travelling showmen were the Irvin family. Before the War, they ran two magnificent Foster engines named *Marvel* and *Marvellous*. Arthur would spend many an hour at local fairs watching them and was more than happy to lend a hand in building up or pulling down the Savage set of gallopers, complete with its great Marenghi organ. This instrument was probably the finest example of any eighty-nine key organ travelling in a three abreast set of gallopers in the country. Charles Marenghi must indeed have been proud of it, for he used to come over from Paris regularly to tune it personally.

In 1939, war came. Arthur was classified as a farmer and thus was in a reserved occupation. Much more of Bridge Farm was turned from dairy to arable. Under the wartime Lease Lend Scheme, a big American-built Case L.A. tractor arrived and this was not only quite capable of ploughing, but coped easily with the new Marshall threshing machine that had by then replaced the Garrett. It was not hard to see that the writing was on the wall for steam, as the new Case saved a man and they, in wartime, were at a premium. Owing to the risk of incendiary bombs, the corn was ricked in the fields and this automatically presented a water problem for the old Wantage, so Arthur let her go, thankful to find a buyer.

She was sold to Wilder's, a firm which, of course, Arthur knew well. In about 1930 they had taken over Paxman's of Clifton Hampden and they also took on their drivers. One of the engines they inherited was a fine single crank compound Burrell, number 2426 of 1901 (which, incidentally, many years later belonged to the author). Its driver was one Tommy Yeo and he was to have not only a great influence on Arthur, but was to become a great friend too. Tommy was a tall, thin man, with a quick turn of phrase and not the type to bear fools gladly. Traction engine driving was, in the main, a hard, tiring and dirty business and Tommy was under no illusions about it. He also knew that a traction engine was, generally speaking, a pretty stout piece of machinery and, provided it was in reasonable condition, it would stand a fair bit of "physic". He would, at times, push an engine very hard indeed, but with no ill effect, for he knew perfectly well what he was doing. With the benefit of hindsight, it can be seen that Tommy's methods were to stand Arthur in good stead later on, when what was called for was a spectacular bit of engine driving to catch the imagination of the public.

Arthur went miles with Tommy Yeo and he was, as often as not, allowed to drive. One day, Tommy was letting the old Burrell roll along, when one of the crosshead slide bars started to get hot. Refusing any entreaty to stop and use the oil can, he simply took the top off and flung the contents in the direction of the overheating part! Of course, it did the trick just as well.

During the War, they were passing through the pretty riverside village of Clifton Hampden, when the Burrell began to get low on water. Tommy spied the A.R.P. water tank, which was installed in all villages against incendiaries. They thought no-one was looking and got the engine filled up. Later that night they went into *The Barley Mow* for a pint and the landlord fixed Tommy with an accusing glare. "I saw you Yeo," he said haughtily, "I saw you!" "What do you reckon you saw?" said Tommy angrily. "I saw you pinching water that's there to protect our village. You've completely emptied our tank." "Well," replied Tommy, "the best thing you can do is to fill it back up, as we're through here again next week!"

Arthur with the American Case L.A. tractor that made his beloved Wantage redundant. From the collection of Arthur Napper.

Arthur and his father. From Arthur Napper's collection.

Tommy had no respect for anybody and could put down his so-called superiors with a delightful turn of phrase. One day he and Arthur were taking the old Burrell and the threshing set out to Long Wittenham, when, rounding the sharp bend out of Appleford, a young schoolmistress came up on the inside, causing Arthur to take violent action with the steering wheel to avoid her. The result was that the last load, which was the elevator, failed to negotiate the bend and dropped into the ditch. This completely blocked the road. A few moments later along came a 'toff' in a bull-nosed Morris. Arthur always remembers that he was wearing plus fours and a deer stalker hat. "Now come along my man," he boomed at Tommy, "clear that engine out of the way at once, I'm in a hurry and I want to get to Abingdon."

"First of all," said Tommy, fixing him with a steely glare, "I am not your man and for another thing I should try a bit of hedge-hopping if you want to get to Abingdon and finally, seeing as it was one bloody silly motorist who put us in the ditch, it's going to be another bloody silly motorist who is going to watch us get it out!"

Tommy could at times be highly impatient and on one occasion it was to cost him his transport home. He had left his bicycle leaning against the front of the engine. He climbed up onto the footplate and made to open the regulator. One of the threshing gang had a slight speech impediment and saw what was about to happen. "T-T-T-Tommy, d-d-don't." "I haven't got time to listen to you," he snapped back and flung the regulator wide open. That was the end of the bike!

The Burrell's tubes were beginning to get a bit thin and had started leaking, so it was decided to run her back into Wilder's for a new set. Tommy had a wry sense of humour and on the journey to Wallingford he kept on suggesting to Arthur that he didn't think she was going to make it and even tried to get Arthur to believe that she was on the point of blowing up. All of a sudden there was indeed an almighty bang, followed by a relatively small cloud of steam. Tommy had put a flask of coffee down on top of the boiler and it was this that had exploded, to their mutual consternation!

When they got to Wilder's yard they were surprised to see the replacement engine standing in the yard with steam up. This was none other than Marshall single, number 37690, destined to become probably the most famous traction engine of them all. Being a Sunday, Tommy was none too keen to do a return trip and he protested violently about this job being foisted on him with no prior warning.

He took out his anger on the new engine and drove her along at a cracking pace. He hadn't driven a Marshall before and mistook the water lift for the injector, which resulted in the feed water getting warm and the inevitable failure of the injector.

They were approaching a down gradient and Arthur suggested that they stop and top up the boiler by means of the pump, but Tommy was in such a vile temper by then that he said "If this bloody old engine drops the plug, then Wilder's can come out in the morning and put it right. It'll teach 'em to make me work on a Sunday."

On this occasion though, Arthur had got thoroughly fed up and when they finally got back he said to Tommy "That's it, I've had more than enough, I shall never drive an engine again as long as I live, with you or with anyone else." With that he stormed off.

The next morning the old Marshall was standing in the yard with steam up, ready to start the day's threshing. There was no-one in sight, so Arthur climbed up onto the footplate and let her run over gently. He was watching her working when a voice said softly "Who said he was never going to drive an engine again?" Behind a low brick wall stood Tommy!

By 1949, the combine harvester had arrived on most of the larger farms and those that still used threshing machines sought the easier method of tractors to drive them. Wilder's was no exception and the wharf at Wallingford became a graveyard of old engines.

Arthur quite vividly recalls the morning that he woke up and thought to himself, If somebody doesn't do something soon, there won't be a traction engine left in Berkshire. There and then he got into his car and went down to Wilder's yard. "You can have any one you like for fifty quid," said John Wilder. "I'll bid you forty-five," countered Arthur. "Done," said John and Marshall number 37690 changed hands. He was to decide on a name that was to perfectly match its impending new rôle as a nationally-known antique and the name alone was to go a long way towards arousing public interest in Britain's, then, newest sport. He called her *Old Timer*.

Threshing was always thirsty work. Arthur is on the right, with Tommy Yeo next to him. From the collection of Arthur Napper.

26

Chapter Three
Off to See the Races

Just off the winding road that leads from Didcot to Appleford, there are a number of small farms and smallholdings. After the War, one of these came on the market. It had originally belonged to Arthur's grandfather. The new owner was a native of Hertfordshire and had decided, after a hard-fought war as a young fighter pilot, to settle down as a market gardener. The name of the property was changed to *Ladygrove* and the new owner was one Miles Chetwynd-Stapylton.

He was a contemporary of Arthur, about thirty years old, and after the vicissitudes and privations of five long war years, he was out to enjoy life. He had everything going for him: he was tall and blonde, with piercing blue eyes and really only looked on the farm as a therapeutic venture, rather than as sound business, for he had inherited money. As an Old Etonian he was indeed a very eligible bachelor, but although it is known that he dallied with a number of local ladies, he never married. Arthur is wisely reticent about going into further detail, but he and Miles became close friends and confidants.

Miles had a charming, if upper crust, sense of humour and this could come out in the most unexpected circumstances. He had once confided to Arthur that he was seeing a certain married lady and Arthur had warned him repeatedly that there would be all hell let loose if the husband ever found out.

Some time later, a breathless Miles burst into Bridge Farm with the news that he had indeed been caught out by the furious husband. "Whatever did you do?" asked Arthur. "Well, he asked me what my name was," said Miles "and I told him it was Arthur Napper." Despite that little setback, the friendship grew and Miles was to become godfather to Arthur's only daughter, Linda.

Arthur had married, at the age of twenty-one, a Miss Megan Biddle and their only daughter, Linda, was born in 1949, on 9th February, Arthur's own birthday. She is today married and lives in nearby Abingdon. Arthur's marriage was, sadly, not to last and he and Megan parted and were later divorced.

Miles had a passion for old things and old American cars in particular. He also owned a Bentley, which he much enjoyed driving hard and fast round the uncluttered Berkshire lanes. Arthur enjoyed it too and always remembers the time they met an old man out walking his dog. Upon sight of the Bentley, the man picked up the dog and threw it into

Miles Chetwynd-Stapylton, D.F.C. Arthur Napper. From Arthur Napper's
Photograph: copyright Harlip, courtesy collection.
of Mrs. Rose Lloyd.

the ditch, then jumped in after it!

Miles saw the funny side of Arthur saving the Marshall from the scrap-man and went down to Wilder's to get one for himself. Perhaps he thought that it might have its uses on his fourteen acres, but, whatever his reasons, he became the proud owner of Aveling and Porter six n.h.p. single cylinder traction engine, number 8923 of 1918, naming it after his farm, *Ladygrove*. She was originally new to J. Berkely Witon of Faccombe, Hampshire.

Despite his love of mechanical things and his prowess in the air, for which he won the Distinguished Flying Cross, Miles could never really get to grips with steam and Arthur and Tommy Yeo had to do practically everything for him. He seemed nervous and would ring up Arthur in a great panic if the engine were in steam, blurting down the 'phone "Arthur, I think you'd better come over, I think she's blowing up." He once asked Arthur what would happen if the safety valves were to stick. Arthur replied that it would go off with an almighty bang. Miles stepped nimbly to the side of the engine, at which Arthur observed "That's no good, it won't blow round you!"

With the memories of his steam threshing days still fresh, Arthur knew that pubs. had been expressly designed with the thirsty engine driver in mind. The fact that Miles and Arthur were simply joy-riding in their newly-acquired charges made no difference and villagers soon got quite used to the sight of one or other engine relaxing in one of the neighbouring villages. Any hint at eccentricity could as often as not be allayed by Miles' generosity, for it was not unusual for him to buy a round for the entire pub.

Miles was a Tory of the old school, but Dick Blackwell, his helper with the engine, was politically 'right across the floor of the House'. Astonished landlords would witness the most amazing scenes between these two and, on occasion, Arthur used to say "I don't know anything about it, I'm neutral and I vote Liberal." The three were always the best of friends, however, and such arguments as there were, were soon forgotten in the common interest in steam.

So here there were two men from totally different backgrounds, yet with a mutual joy of living and a fervent desire to save the traction engine from total oblivion, when fate decided it was time to step in.

One summer's evening in July 1950, Arthur decided to take a stroll up to *The Carpenter's Arms* in the village and join Miles for a drink. They both enjoyed a game of billiards and when the game was over, the subject of engines inevitably came up. "You know, Arthur," said Miles, "that old engine of mine is faster than yours." "I know damn well it's not" replied Arthur. Being the more knowledgeable in steam matters, he countered with the suggestion that the Marshall was sprung fore and aft and had probably been new to a haulier, in which case it would have been geared accordingly. All this fell on deaf ears and Miles would have none of it. "Well, there's only one way to settle the matter once and for all, we'll have a race," said Arthur. "That's a darned good idea," agreed Miles. "What are we going to race for? After all, I shall want a prize for winning" he grinned. "I know," he suggested, after a moment's thought, "we'll race for a firkin of ale: nine gallons of beer." "You're on" said Arthur excitedly.

The date was set for a fortnight later, Sunday 30th July, 1950 and the two protagonists were to be on the front meadow at Bridge Farm by eleven a.m. The intervening couple of weeks gave them both the ideal opportunity to visit all the local pubs. to drum up supporters and generally publicise the gladiatorial fight to the finish.

In the main, the locals saw no more in it than they would have done in an inter-village tug of war. This was just something a little bit different. Around Didcot the bets were on Miles, but over at Sutton Courtenay and Appleford, Arthur was their man.

Tommy and Miles took *Ladygrove* over the preceding evening and parked for the night at the local blacksmith's. This was due to leaking tubes, which did not auger well for the morrow. The following morning, steam was raised early and at the appointed time, the two engines rumbled their way into the long meadow in front of Bridge Farm.

Miles, never over-confident as an engine driver, had asked Tommy Yeo to do the honours and had decided he would steer, but at the last moment Tommy dropped out, knowing what the outcome was likely to be. He confided to Arthur later "I wasn't going to stand up there and be made a fool of, especially as I practically taught you to drive an engine in the first place." Miles had to make a second choice and settled for Bill Cross, another local driver. Arthur was of course to drive *Old Timer*, no-one that day would have torn him from the footplate. It was he who had thrown down the gauntlet and no-one was going to savour the victory more than Arthur. He chose as his steersman, the local coal merchant, Freddy Owen.

Gradually people began to arrive at the scene of battle. Many were on foot, one or two came by car and quite a few pedalled in from the other villages on the only means of transport they had. Some, later prominent in the engine movement, were to claim in later years that they, too, were there, but this was not so. It was an entirely locals only affair.

The two drivers stoked their steeds and viewed each other from their respective footplates. The day was sultry and windless and two columns of acrid black smoke rose lazily from the chimneys, as the engines stood abreast for the start.

There was a slight delay, as two of Arthur's farm lads had to herd the cattle away to safety. Meanwhile, the two marker men walked away up the meadow to take up position. The race was to be up the field, round the two men and back to the start; about half a mile. *Old Timer* was by this time blowing off and raring to go, but *Ladygrove*, with its wide, cast-iron, Burrell chimney, was not steaming well at all.

"Get ready," shouted someone in the small crowd of onlookers, "Get set," shouted someone else and "GO," they all chorused. With an almighty clang from the gearing, Bill Cross threw the old Aveling wide open and, with a staccato roar from the chimney, *Ladygrove* was away. Arthur cursed audibly. *Old Timer* stood rooted to the spot and just wheezed embarrassingly from her glands. Arthur slammed her into reverse and she delivered two or three apologetic puffs and went; backwards! Miles and Bill glanced behind them and saw what had happened. "Come on Arthur," yelled Miles, "what are you playing at? Make a race of it!" he chortled.

"I'll make a race of it alright," muttered Arthur between clenched teeth, as he heaved the reverse into foregear and gave her the works. Roaring a solid column of black smoke, soot, sparks and cinders vertically into the sky, *Old Timer* wreaked her revenge. Never before had the fifty year old engine been driven so hard. The exhaust was a continuous roar, like some jet aircraft taking off, and the motionwork had blurred into invisibility. I'll show him who's going to make a race of it, thought Arthur, as he thundered past Miles at over ten miles an hour.

It was now his turn to look over his shoulder and to his great amusement, *Ladygrove* seemed unwilling to keep up. Arthur looked again in disbelief. She had stopped. She had run out of steam! The sudden demand on the boiler, already with leaking tubes and a sluggish fire, had proved too much. Arthur closed the regulator and gently reversed back to the ailing antagonist. "Are we going to have a race Miles," asked Arthur triumphantly, "or would you prefer a tow?" Miles and Bill glared back defiantly. Bill set about getting some steam in the Aveling, whilst Miles got down to put the blower on. After a while, *Ladygrove* recovered and they decided to make it a race for the rest of the way. With the exhausts roaring in unison, the engines sailed round the two marker men at the top end of the field, then they were in the home straight.

History in the making: the two regulators were thrown wide open on Sunday July 30th, 1950 and with gears clanging and steam and smoke roaring from the two chimneys, Britain's then-newest sport was born. From Arthur Napper's collection.

The two old ladies thundered back towards the farm, straining every steel sinew. Eight great iron-shod wheels bit into the turf as the two furious monsters battled it out. It was Arthur who shut off steam first, to the cheers of the little crowd, with Miles, sheepishly, ten seconds behind him. "Everyone up to the pub., the beer's on me," shouted Miles gallantly and, as if not to be left out, the two old engines went as well.

That it had been a jolly good bit of sport, everyone was agreed. What they had witnessed had been some high drama, every bit as spectacular as anything seen at a race meeting and all at only ten miles an hour. Arthur's mother watched the departing engines and muttered, to no-one in particular, "There's either something about that old engine, or there's something about our Arthur." How right she was.

Although the original bet had been for a firkin of ale, in fact it never materialised, yet Miles, magnanimous in defeat, bought drinks for all-comers, so it was indeed a wager for ale.

Whatever would a rally organiser say today if only twenty-five people turned up? From this tiny knot of spectators, back in the summer of 1950, was to grow the vast rally movement as we know it today. From the collection of Arthur Napper.

Miles wasn't entirely satisfied that justice had been done, however, and felt that the leaking tubes and the poor steaming had affected the outcome. His lack of knowledge hid the real reason for his defeat. It was, of course, simply the gear ratios on the two engines which made it a foregone conclusion, although Arthur was far more ready to throw

32

caution to the winds and push his Marshall to the limit. The two engines rested in the car park of *The Carpenter's Arms* while the honours were done within. Arthur remembers being brought down to earth with a bump, when later, much later, that afternoon, he had to go and feed and muck out over one hundred pigs!

Miles retired to consider his next move. Re-tubing, he thought, would cure *Ladygrove*'s shy performance and Wilder's duly carried out the work. A fresh coat of paint, he considered, wouldn't look amiss either and that completed, she would be as good as new and ready to take on anything. Another race? Well, why not?

"Same time, same place," laughed Arthur, "so long as you buy the beer." "I shan't need to this time," grinned Miles. Not to be outdone, Arthur decided that *Old Timer* could do with smartening up and she too was repainted and the famous wooden nameplate attached to the front of the chimney.

Sunday August 20th, 1950 was the date set for the re-run. This time it was a cloudless summer day and so confident was Arthur that, like a boxer coming out of his corner, he decided to take *Old Timer* up the village street to meet his adversary.

An article in the *Didcot Advertiser* ensured that what had begun as a small handful of people, became a crowd of over two hundred and fifty as the morning wore on at Bridge Farm.

At 11.29 precisely, Bert Faulkner brought down the white flag and the engines were off. Two solid columns of black smoke poured into the morning sky and the sun glinted off the fresh green paint and polished brass. This time the crowd really joined in the spirit of the occasion, yelling encouragement at their favoured driver. "Come on Arthur," shouted some, "let her have it" and, with the regulator wide open, he did just that. "Go on Miles, give her the works!" yelled the Didcot contingent, some just managing to keep up, by running as hard as they could.

The Old Aveling was giving a pretty fair account of herself and this time was steaming well. Bill Cross had noticed Arthur's tactics and realised that if he was to have any hope of winning, he must keep steam at all costs. Arthur, of course, knew this too and had a really heavy fire going, so heavy in fact that coal was rolling back onto the footplate. He knew that this was the only way that the boiler could possibly cope with the demand for steam that was to be made upon it. Full regulator continuously for over half a mile, had not be catered for in the design office at either Gainsborough or Rochester!

In just under five minutes it was again Arthur who shut off steam first, to much cheering and many triumphant blasts on the whistle. It was, however, a closer run thing, with Miles just two lengths behind, but the gear ratios once again were the deciding factor. "I think this is going to be an expensive morning" said Miles, as he surveyed the sizeable crowd of onlookers. "Never mind, everyone up to the pub., the beer's on me." The two engines headed a procession to a very lively *Carpenter's Arms.*

Under starter's orders for the second race. 11.29 a.m., Sunday 20th August, 1950. From Arthur Napper's collection.

One of the merry crowd was the flag man, Bert Faulkner, who was one of the thirty-two children of the late John Faulkner, the jockey, and so was forged a connection, albeit slight, between the two famous racing sons of Appleford. Bert Faulkner was a great character, with a particular penchant for standing on his head! He would lay bets, always for beer, on a variety of stunts, to be performed upside down. Arthur remembers being rendered speechless, when he walked round the corner of the pub. to find him standing on his head on the rim of *Old Timer's* flywheel! Perhaps sensing that the regulator was none too secure, he had taken the precaution of tying the flywheel to the steering wheel with string; just in case! It became an Appleford tradition, for the next few years at least, to head the grand parade at the rallies with a man walking in front, holding aloft a red flag. That man was Bert Faulkner.

Arthur acknowledges the cheering crowd at the end of the second race. This time one vital ingredient was present: the press. From the collection of Arthur Napper.

Miles, the loser for the second time, steers *Ladygrove* in the direction of *The Carpenter's Arms*. Photograph: courtesy of Mrs. Rose Lloyd.

"Have a drink Miles." The victor and the vanquished. From the collection of Arthur Napper.

"Give the old girl a drink" yelled some, whilst others thought, What a waste! Arthur celebrates victory at *The Carpenter's Arms*. From Arthur Napper's collection.

So two grand races had been run, resulting in two jolly good sessions at *The Carpenter's*. Arthur and Miles had enjoyed it, so too had the locals, for whom it had provided a novel diversion on a Sunday morning and the landlord of the pub. had done a roaring trade. That, conceivably, could have been the end of the story but for one other person who was present. His name was 'Chick' Fowler and he was a journalist.

Quite by chance he had reported the first race in the *Didcot Advertiser* and on hearing of the re-run, he had decided to alert the *Daily Mirror*. August was, and is, always known as the silly season, because so many of the newsworthy people are on holiday, that the press will go almost anywhere to get a story. This one looked promising and was right in the tradition of the English love of eccentricity. It would do as a good pot boiler. A reporter and a photographer were duly sent along and when the race was over, they persuaded Arthur to give the engine a drink, by pouring a gallon of beer down the chimney! "What a waste" muttered someone in the crowd, "that would have done us more good."

On Monday 21st August the story broke nationally entitled "Arthur's engine wins the big race – at 10 m.p.h." Engine lovers everywhere were to realise that there could be a future for the old and discarded machines. Arthur knew how to handle the press and, having given them an awe-inspiring performance at the regulator of *Old Timer*, he went on to admit even to being in love with the thing, that he would never part with it and would make sure that it was looked after when he was gone. These were just the sort of sentiments for which the press was looking. Arthur's mother, however, was none too pleased to read that Arthur had once run away from home and joined a firm of travelling showmen, a story which was totally without foundation. She was so angry that at one point she considered taking legal action against the *Mirror*.

Slowly, Arthur began to realise that he was on to something with tremendous possibilities. Interested people began to get in touch and if they did nothing else, at least they enjoyed talking about engines.

Arthur was a steam man through and through, Miles was not. Although he had played, unwittingly, a tremendous rôle in challenging Arthur, his heart wasn't really in it. Very gradually, Arthur and Miles were to drift apart, with more and more of Arthur's time and energy being taken up by the new-found hobby that had suddenly materialised. As a farmer in a big way, Arthur had a thorough grasp of the fickle economics of agriculture and was, from the outset of their friendship, more than a little worried about Miles' ability to make his smallholding a financial success. Time and again he urged him not to diversify, as the farm was too small. Miles dabbled in all aspects: a few chickens, a few pigs, cattle and barely enough arable to make Arthur's annual threshing visits worthwhile. "Go for one thing in a big way" begged Arthur, but Miles took no notice. The Lord loves a cheerful giver, the Good Book tells us and Miles, as we have seen, was certainly that, but he was forced eventually to sell up and move to a tiny cottage in Long Wittenham. His health started to deteriorate and the woman with whom he was living ultimately deserted him. For a time he took a job as a personnel officer with Morris Motors at Oxford, a post for which Arthur imagines he would have been ideally suited, for above all things he was kind and understanding. For one reason or another, however, the good times seemed over and it came as a tremendous shock to Arthur to learn that Miles had, one night, shot his dog and then turned the gun on himself.

Miles' contribution can be seen to be inestimable. Without him there would have been no challenge and without that, no race. How exactly the traction engine movement would have progressed is anybody's guess, but it would probably have been a far more restrained affair and very much more rooted in museums. The fate of *Ladygrove* too is sad.

Miles sold her to some Gloucestershire timber merchants called Bourne, who removed her front nearside wheel to enable her to drive a saw bench. Arthur tried vainly to buy her back, but they wanted silly money and in the end she was cut up for scrap. Still, she had done sterling work in laying the foundations of the movement and the results were starting to show.

Somebody had the presence of mind to cut out the *Mirror* article and send it to a consultant eye surgeon living at Bray in Berkshire. His name was Giles Romanes and he became tremendously excited by what he read, for he too owned a traction engine. One evening in February 1951, he rang Arthur up and they arranged to meet. Giles duly went over to Bridge Farm and the two men hit it off from the start. He hailed originally from Dunmow in Essex, where he had been fascinated, from his earliest years, by the steam threshing sets that abounded in that area. His medical work took him to hospitals in Reading and Maidenhead and the Queen Victoria Hospital at East Grinstead in Sussex. In 1948, whilst living near Reading, he discovered a Wallis and Steevens traction engine lying out of use in a depot near Dummer. Her number was 7683 of 1919 and she had last worked for the Hampshire War Agricultural Committee. Her driver had been one Don Wootton and he had named the engine after his daughter, Eileen. Giles purchased the engine for the, then, princely sum of fifty pounds.

During his time at Appleford, Giles threw down the gauntlet and challenged Arthur to yet another race. They agreed that it might be mutually convenient to find a venue halfway between their two homes and a glance at the map showed the Oxfordshire village of Nettlebed to be about so. The two of them went out in the car to try and find a suitable field and found what they were looking for on the northern outskirts of the village. The question then arose as to who owned it. Opposite was a row of cottages and Giles, who is an Old Etonian, recalls with amusement that he asked Arthur to go and knock on the door, "as with my accent they'll think there's something up!" Lord Nuffield, the motor car magnate, was the owner, but the field was let to a tenant farmer, who readily gave his permission for them to race in the field.

The weekend prior to the agreed date, not two, but three engines set forth for Nettlebed, for Giles had decided to bring his newly-acquired McLaren tractor, number 1837 of 1936, along for good measure and asked his friend, Len Kingdom, to drive it over for him. Len, incidentally, had been a stoker on a sailing ship at one time. If that sounds like a contradiction in terms, the ship was indeed powered by sail, but on board was a small boiler and donkey engine to assist in loading cargo.

It was when the two engines arrived in Henley and stopped for water that the fun started. The Police arrived and started questioning Len as to their destination. He stalled them for as long as he could, but having decided that all was in order, they turned their attention to Giles. Behind *Eileen* he was towing a four-wheeled traction waggon, upon which was mounted a motorbike for their homeward journey. "Hallo, hallo, hallo," boomed one officer, in traditional music hall style, "what have we got here? That there motorcycle is not agricultural equipment, neither is it for the needs of the locomotive," he concluded with authority. "In which case I propose to summons you for the offence in question." Giles' heart sank, but no number of protestations seemed to make any difference to the officious policeman. On learning that there was in fact another engine on the road, heading for Nettlebed from the opposite direction, the two eager officers leapt into their car, hellbent on procuring a further prosecution. When they arrived at the field, Arthur had beaten them to it by a very narrow margin and was off the road when they arrived. They almost threatened to summons him at the first opportunity!

Sunday 21st June, 1951 dawned clear and bright, a real English summer's day. Anything new is a gift to the press and Giles had had no difficulty in gaining the co-operation of the local papers to promote the event. The resultant publicity brought out probably the first model traction engine to attend an outdoor event. It was called *Winifred* and had been built by the late Tom Fisher of Earley, who at one time had worked for Tasker's of Andover. He had discovered the small locomotive type boiler under a bench in the works.

Over a thousand people lined the route down the field, but at the appointed time of eleven a.m., Arthur and *Old Timer* still had no steam. The crowd waited impatiently to see what would happen. In the end there was nothing for it but to throw the fire out and start again. Giles shovelled out half of his fire, which formed the basis of the new one in *Old Timer*'s firebox. With a fresh supply of good coal, *Old Timer* quickly got up steam and by 11.45 all was nearly ready, with the two engines abreast at the line and safety valves at full stretch.

Someone in the crowd then realised that their host, Lord Nuffield, was also present, so he was invited to act as judge for the contest. Mrs. B.W. Rycroft, wife of Giles' chief, Benjamin (later Sir Benjamin) Rycroft, did the honours and brought down the flag. Once again with an almighty clang, the two engines sprang into action. The course was, as usual, down the field and back, having negotiated an electricity pylon at the far end. Both engines were at full regulator as the crowd cheered and shouted. Arthur's experience told immediately. A very heavy fire was essential, he knew, as most of it would roar out of the chimney and plenty of oil for the bearings was needed. Arthur and his steersman, Dick Blackwell, surged ahead and it soon became obvious what the outcome was going to be. *Eileen* was losing steam pressure as she rounded the pylon, then to cap it all a crankshaft bearing started to get hot. Giles simply had to stop and oil it, by which time Arthur, with much victorious whistling, had crossed the finishing line. Giles and his steersman, Fred Ham, a medical friend from Windsor, trailed in a minute or so later. *Eileen* showed the result of her exertions, with a set of very leaky tubes.

"They're all awa' – true beat full power" wrote Kipling and indeed they were at Nettlebed on Sunday June 21st, 1951. Photograph: copyright Times Newspapers Ltd., courtesy of Giles Romanes.

This time, however, the wager was carried out to the letter. Giles had made arrangements with the landlord of *The Bull Inn* in Nettlebed and a firkin of ale had duly been set up in the bar for all to enjoy at Giles' expense. Arthur remained unbeaten. During the wait for *Old Timer* to get up steam, someone, it is not recorded who, had the bright idea of making a collection for a hospital charity and, incredibly, the total was some eighty pounds. Here, for the first time, was a glimpse of the charitable potential of the traction engine rally. Today, of course, charity and the traction engine go hand in hand and since 1951 the sums raised for all manner of causes must run into millions.

Although Arthur was well-aware of the Police interest in the proceedings, it was pure coincidence, not a protective measure, that his mate, Dick Blackwell, was himself a Police officer, at Didcot. On the way home, once again victorious, they spent too long in one of the Wallingford pubs. and it began to grow dark. Arthur decided to run the engine onto the side of the road for the night. A Police colleague from Long Wittenham happened to be on hand to direct them. Arthur and Dick didn't realise that at the crucial moment he was standing right in front of the smokebox. Arthur opened the regulator and promptly knocked him flat!

"My goodness," said Arthur, "what with Giles in trouble with them at Henley and now me running them over at Wallingford, we aren't getting off to a very good start!"

Arthur and *Old Timer* storm into the home straight to win by a good five lengths. The Wallis, *Eileen*, was suffering from an overheated bearing and a set of very leaky tubes. Photograph: copyright Times Newspapers Ltd., courtesy of Giles Romanes.

Giles' case duly came up before the Henley Bench and although the general feeling was that the Police were being pernickety, the magistrates felt it a duty to back up the local constabulary and he was summarily fined five pounds. The matter, however, did not entirely rest there, as the mighty *Sunday Times* not only thought that the Oxfordshire Police were tiny-minded, but came out and said so. The article in the *Maidenhead Weekly* ran a headline that delighted Giles: "Eileen the erring". There and then he changed the name of the engine and *Eileen the Erring* she is to this day.

Eileen was incidentally, the very first traction engine ever seen by the author as a small boy in 1955, hauling a load of hay towards Maidenhead and it fired his imagination, as it did many many others, in those early years. Giles' other engine, the little McLaren tractor, only came over to Nettlebed for the joy of it and it occurs to me that were Giles not the absolute gentleman that he is, he might have used it to challenge Arthur, in which case, with its high three-speed gearing, the result would have been very different!

This time the wager was carried out to the letter. Giles and Arthur sample the first pints in *The Bull*. Photograph: copyright Times Newspapers Ltd., courtesy of Giles Romanes.

"Well done, Giles" says Lord Nuffield at the end of the Nettlebed race.
Photograph: copyright Times Newspapers Ltd., courtesy of Giles Romanes.

The losing engine and her supporters. L. to r. Joe Kingdom, David Smith,
Fred Ham, Giles Romanes, Tom Fisher and G. Derman. Photograph: copyright
Norman Greville, courtesy of Giles Romanes.

Giles Romanes' little McLaren tractor at Nettlebed. From the collection of Arthur Napper.

Winifred was the first model traction engine to attend an outdoor steam event. Photograph: Giles Romanes.

45

Chapter Four
They're All Awa'!

Back in 1893, an organisation was formed which, eventually, called itself The National Traction Engine and Tractor Association Incorporated. It was, in fact, an organisation with the aim of promoting and protecting the rights of the growing number of traction engine users. When one realises that at the turn of the century, the only mechanical machine to be encountered on public roads was a steam engine, its rôle was of phenomenal importance. In country districts there was enough opposition to railways disturbing the peace of the countryside, but to have to endure great snorting monsters right in the village itself was just too much for many of the populace. In a way their point of view can be appreciated. It could be a dangerous experience to meet an engine with a nervous horse in the shafts of one's carriage, so frightening the horses was a crime which many a village policeman found quite easy to prove satisfactorily to the local magistrates. It must be remembered too that the peace of the countryside in those days meant exactly that. There was no noise of any sort, which is almost impossible to imagine today, as even the most out-of-the-way places suffer the abuse of heavy lorries and the din of modern farm implements.

The law was stacked against the traction engine owner. How a traction engine was supposed to "consume its own smoke" has never been properly defined, but the law said that it had to, so one shovelful too many on the fire and the ever vigilant bobby would swing into action again. "The engine was emitting smoke on the highway," he would intone to the Bench and nine times out of ten His Worship would nod solemnly in agreement. Taxation laws varied from one county to the next. In some counties you could only travel during the hours of daylight, in others, progress was only legal after dark. Thomas Aveling once angrily pointed out, regarding damage to bridges, "If a team of horses takes a load over a bridge and that bridge collapses, the carter has nothing to pay, but if one of my engines takes the same load over that bridge and the load damages it, the driver has everything to pay." Not a few unexplained fires were put down to the passing of a traction engine and claims for damage to property, even washing besmirched by smoke, were certainly not unknown.

It can thus be seen that The National Traction Engine and Tractor Association had plenty to keep it busy. In 1905, it widened its sphere of interest and incorporated The National Threshing Machine Owners

Association and The Steam Cultivation Development Association. That it was a body of some influence can be judged by its prestigious headquarters, which were in Duke Street Chambers, Reading. Rather delightfully, telegrams were to be dispatched to "Threshaul" Reading, when in need of assistance!

By 1952, however, things had run seriously into decline. The advent of the motorcar and motor lorry meant that mechanical transport was no longer a once-weekly novelty on empty roads. The village policeman too had a lot more to think about; speed for instance; and once steam threshing sets, ploughing tackle and showmen had started to hold up the traffic, it was often more prudent to let the engine get on with it, rather than compound the problem by stopping it for some misdemeanour. Private insurance was also available by then, which made most help that could be offered by a friendly society rather superfluous.

By the early 'fifties, the Association was practically a lost cause, firstly because no-one was using traction engines to any great extent and secondly because those that were, were far less harassed legally.

The Association's General Secretary in 1952 was one Frank Stephens and he got to hear of Arthur's activities with great interest. Perhaps hoping for a new lease of life for his ailing Association, he went over to Appleford and offered Arthur a fund of help and advice. His experience of problems arising at agricultural shows was to prove invaluable in organising the first rally of traction engines, staged at Bridge Farm on Sunday June 8th, 1952. True, the word rally was not used; Frank Stephen's publicity heralded it as the North Berkshire Traction Engine Race; but a rally it was nonetheless, as apart from the competing engines, there were some who just came over to put their engines on show and, for the very first time, an engine in full showman's livery was to make its appearance, complete with canopy lights and twisted brass cab supports.

The *Daily Mail* published the story on Monday 9th June and reported the event in horse racing parlance: "Ten ton horse beats field in the half mile". A far superior eye-witness account of the proceedings was subsequently penned by the late Michael Salmon and printed in The Road Locomotive Society Journal. This was his impression:

"We turned off the Oxford Road and knew we were right, for there were well-defined marks of strakes on the road to guide us. Well outside the village, though, we were held up in a traffic jam and then realised, to our amazement, that we were on the end of a queue about a quarter of a mile long for the car park. Slowly wending our way through the crowds past the race field, it seemed more like an enormous fair. A first

47

aid tent, a tea tent, own risk notices and literally THOUSANDS OF PEOPLE. Reliable estimates were from five to ten thousand and there were we just expecting a dozen or so owners and their friends!

Leaving the car, we were just in time to see the grand parade leaving the farm yard, where steam had been raised, and passing to the race field. First a man in front, complete with top hat, tails and red flag. Then a four-inch-scale model traction engine from Earley, near Reading, followed by a tiny Wallis three ton tractor on strakes, her driver taller than her funnel. Dwarfing her was Mr. Esmond Kimbell's fine Marshall traction engine, with that enormously solid look of a big Marshall. But now, shade your eyes, lest you be quite dazzled by the brass and varnish of Mr. Wharton's Burrell showman's engine; painted, lined, lettered and polished to perfection and running like a clock on her pressed-on rubbers. Painted ladies they may have been called, but that is as may be, I could go for that one in a big way! The resident Marshall, Mr. Napper's *Old Timer*, followed, with a Wallis expansion behind her, a Foden tractor, kept in fine order by Mr. Ian Woollett, was graciously adjusting her pace to the iron-shod wheels ahead and an Aveling and a second Wallis expansion brought up the rear. A fine sight they made, but it was impossible to see them all at once owing to the people surging round.

The gate to the race field was small and awkward, but plenty of coarse gravel had been laid in case of rain. It was, nevertheless, a credit to the drivers that no engine needed two goes at it and none of the spectators was run over.

The five traction engines lined up to race and the four others were put on show on one side. Photography was impossible owing to the crowds and colour would have been essential when the showman's engine started driving the lights and scores of coloured bulbs under her canopy lit up her gleaming motionwork.

Then, "They're Off!" Five regulators pushed wide open, five funnels belching, ten safety valves lifting, away they went down the long, smooth, green field with a railway embankment at the end.

Surely a better field for the purpose could not have been found in all Berkshire? As they turned at the far end it seemed they must collide, but no, back they came, *Kim* in the lead until a hot crankshaft bearing told and *Old Timer* drew away just at the last to win by a few yards.

Ten excited men mopped their faces and within a few minutes, ten safety valves lifted again, the old engines were game for more! A little rain fell and the state of the Foden can be judged, for several elegantly dressed ladies were seen to take shelter in her cab. Then four non-competing engines went for a parade around the field and the Foden and the Burrell had an impromptu race which the Foden won, of course, but

48

that Burrell sure can go! As the rain increased the crowds departed, but the enthusiasts remained, among them a man who had left home at five that morning to bring a party of friends to the race in his Sentinel S type steam waggon.

Gradually the party broke up, some left to drive their engines home, others to load *Kim* onto a trailer for her long ride back to the Midlands, many to drive hundreds of miles in plebeian petrol motor cars and at least one to fly away in his own aeroplane! Such was the scene at Appleford in 1952, a grand show and the thanks of thousands are due to Mr. Napper and his friends for staging it."

Painted ladies they may have been called, but Jack Wharton's Burrell showman's engine enthralled the crowd at Appleford in 1952. It was the first time an engine in full showman's livery had attended a steam event and it is still attending rallies regularly. From Arthur Napper's collection.

Such then was one man's impression of England's very first traction engine rally. For the record, the competing engines were as follows:

Marshall number 37690, *Old Timer*   Arthur Napper
Wallis and Steevens number 7683, *Eileen the Erring*   Giles Romanes

Marshall eight n.h.p. G.P., *Kim*	Esmond Kimbell
Wallis and Steevens number 7293, *Pandora*	Quick Brothers
Aveling and Porter number 8923	Miles Chetwynd-Stapylton.

The non-competing engines were:

Burrell six n.h.p. showman's engine	S.J. Wharton
Wallis and Steevens number 7370	W.H. Tame
Foden D type tractor	Ian Woollett
Wallis and Steevens three ton tractor	Giles Romanes
Sentinel S type tipper waggon	Dick Woolley.

Arthur, wearing the familiar trilby hat, gives *Old Timer* the works at Appleford in 1952. From the collection of Arthur Napper.

Perhaps the most amazing thing about the event was the appearance of the Sentinel, all the way from the Welsh Marches and back in the day! Dick Woolley was still using her for haulage of road stone at that time and apparently thought nothing of using her for a day trip to Berkshire!

Arthur Wallis, of Wallis and Steevens' of Basingstoke, was, incredibly, one of the spectators and presented Arthur with an inscribed silver salver for, yet again, winning the race. That gift he still treasures.

The tea tent referred to in Michael Salmon's account was very swiftly turned into the beer tent, so that the customary firkin of ale could be dispensed. One of the local Police, who had been called out to direct the traffic, turned barman for the occasion.

Esmond Kimbell, a plant and machinery contractor from Northampton, had issued the challenge for the race and had in fact bought the big eight n.h.p. Marshall specially for the event. He had it low-loaded all the way from Northampton, as a piece of free publicity for The National Agricultural Contractors Association. The fleet of engines that he had operated before the War, all carried a motif in the shape of a bell, with the word Kim set within it. This was, of course, a play on his name.

He once offered to compare for Arthur the controls of a traction engine and those of a light aircraft and took Arthur for a flight. All of a sudden an R.A.F. jet zoomed up at them from the nearby base at Abingdon, giving them both a hair-raising few moments. Arthur stuck to driving engines after that.

The 1952 rally at Appleford was to see the end of flat racing. Although it was indeed a fantastic sight and the sound of five single cylinder engines at full bore must have been music indeed, one or two engineers had begun to tut-tut and shake their heads. The problem was not whether any damage might be caused to the boilers of the engines, but whether the flywheels would continue to stand the strain. They were, after all, made of cast iron and were one to burst, the consequences would have been catastrophic. It would certainly have killed the steersman, who would have been directly in the line of fire and great chunks of cast iron suddenly hurled into an unsuspecting crowd of people was not only highly undesirable, but the damage to the reputation of the infant engine movement would also have been disastrous.

It was felt too that the amount of preparation involved in getting an engine to attend just one race was too much and the public also felt strongly that some of the journeys they made were not warranted by five minutes' worth of spectacle.

One or two people actually put pen to paper on the matter and Giles Romanes received a letter from an outraged landlord in Southampton, berating him for cruelty to traction engines and taking him to task for misusing them so blatantly!

Frank Stephens, Arthur and the N.T.E. and T. Association

committee put their heads together to resolve the problem. Frank had realised the charitable potential of rallies straight away and admission was subsequently charged for some suitably worthwhile cause. Arthur came up with ideas for various games and competitions to keep the engine driver and public occupied for an entire afternoon, but with the added proviso that none of it would over-tax the engine, thus were thought up some fascinating games of skill. The back to back race, which involved two engines tied together by a thin piece of binder twine, tested the skill of an engine driver to the limit, as if either driver was the slightest bit heavy-handed with the regulator, the string would break. The slow race, where the last engine up the field was the winner, was, again, a great test of skill, as disqualification came if the engine actually stopped. Other tests of a driver's ability included a teeter-totter, or balancing act, where just one turn of the crank would, literally, tip the balance. The engine drivers enjoyed the friendly competition and it gave the public something to watch.

It isn't really any wonder that some of the die-hard steam men were stopped dead in their tracks when they had to witness a scarecrow race, as the dignity of an engine driver was lost for all time. The race involved a series of items of ladies' clothing placed at strategic points up the field and the engine driver had to stop and don the female attire. It was, of course, highly amusing to watch a pot-bellied old gentleman struggling into a bra!

The first obstacle race, in 1953, with Arthur and *Old Timer* crossing the finishing line. From Arthur Napper's collection.

Such games as musical chairs gave a measure of audience participation, to use a horrible modern expression, and a good deal of humour could be introduced by inviting the ladies to try their hand at steering. The ever popular tug o' war showed just how powerful a steam engine could be, but on wet ground, fifty or so assorted human beings would be more than a match for it, to the delight of the cheering onlookers. Moments of high drama could be created by an imaginative commentator and an engine driver with a sense of humour. The author recalls the scene at an early Cranborne Rally, when Walter Edney's single crank compound Burrell was hauled ignominiously backwards out of the ring by six Land Rovers, with Walter unconcernedly reading a newspaper. Right at the very last minute, he turned and nonchalantly touched the double high. Six Land Rovers stopped dead in their tracks. With a wry smile, Walter turned, just touched the regulator and *Marmaduke*, as the engine was known, effortlessly hauled six protesting Land Rovers, with all wheels spinning, right up the arena and out at the far end. It was neat showmanship and just what the public wanted to see.

In the main, the attitude of the press was benign and although they hinted at eccentricity, they never mentioned it outright. "The more futile a sport," intoned the *Observer*, in 1955, "the greater its purity and the enthusiasm of its adherents. As soon as it achieves a purpose, then it becomes vulgar and it acquires an element of brashness in victory or bitterness in defeat." The article went on to extol the virtues of simply doing something for fun. Cassandra in the *Daily Mirror* gave prominence to the fact that Raymond Glendenning, the famous sports commentator, was to open the 1955 rally and the late Mr. Airey Neave, M.P. for Abingdon (later to be so tragically killed) was to present the prizes. For some reason, Cassandra took a hearty dislike to Glendenning arriving by helicopter, which he called a nasty modern bluebottle contraption. They were, of course, the first of many celebrities down the years to gain a useful bit of publicity by doing their stuff at the local traction engine rally.

Another correspondent concluded his report of the 1957 Appleford event "All in all a day out for the purist and not for the red-blooded. Not a single boiler exploded and nobody got run over. These new traction engine buffs seem a safety-conscious bunch". That, from the engine driver's point of view, is just as it should be and in over thirty-five years of engine events, only one person, a small boy who was fooling about, has in fact been killed.

Easter Monday, April 6th, 1953, saw the first event to occur as a consequence of those at Appleford, organised by The Andover and

District Model Engineering Society. They advertised it as a Road Locomotive Rally, not the first time that magic word rally had been used, as Chris Lambert called his steam days a Rally of his Old Gentlemen, well back in the late 'forties. The Andover event was, however, the first of some thirty enjoyable annual events, held at such memorable venues as Finckley Manor Farm and Longparish House. For many years they were always very eagerly awaited, as they were held at the start of the outdoor season in early May, when everyone had had quite enough of the winter. The names of Howell, Pemble and Wicks will always be synonymous with these events. For over twenty years, Arthur was to be an ardent supporter, steaming there and back, a round trip of over one hundred miles.

The north of England was not to be left out of all this excitement and enthusiasts started their own event at Pickering in Yorkshire. Imitating what they had seen and enjoyed at Appleford, they called it a Traction Engine Derby. It was a straightforward flat race. It did for the north what Appleford had done for the south, but the old-time steam diehards once again looked askance at the speed at which the flywheels were turning. They too found the event to be "over too quick" and the more sedate, but nonetheless enjoyable, traction engine rally was soon established.

Twelve engines attended the 1953 Appleford Rally and people came from as far afield as Cornwall, County Durham and even Scotland. The field was laid out in two figures of eight, made of straw bales, and the engines were invited to race, drawing a threshing machine behind them, around the obstacle course. This had the desired effect of keeping the competitive spirit and allowing drivers the chance to give 'em the works for short bursts, but also keeping the revs. down to a safer level. Arthur had himself witnessed the effect of a burst flywheel, when the governor belt broke on a threshing set. The feeder on top of the machine was decapitated.

Having always had a love of the fairground, Arthur decided to rescue one of the dwindling number of showman's engines. He went up to Southall in London to the yard of the famous showlady, the late Miss Sally Beach. She had just pensioned off Burrell tractor number 3497, *May Queen*. The asking price was eighty-five pounds. Arthur, ever the businessman, made a bid of eighty pounds. "I'm not having any of that old nonsense Mr. Napper, because I'm only letting you have it in the first place because I know you won't have it chopped up." Arthur and Giles steamed the little engine home via Giles' house at Bray.

Another firm ready to see the back of steam was Messrs. Whittles of Blackwater, near Camberley. They had for sale a large Fowler class R2,

King Edward. Arthur bought it and took it to the 1954 Andover and Appleford Rallies, subsequently parting with it to an enthusiast at Henley. He called in a boiler inspector, a Mr. Robinson of Oxford, who promptly put his hammer through the plate just behind the smokebox. The author recalls hearing the tale many years ago from Robinson himself. He ended with the opinion "If anyone tells me that a paper bag will hold two hundred pounds of steam, I won't call him a liar." Almost unbelievably, today, the owner considered that the game certainly wasn't worth the candle and the engine was cut up. The traction engine was far from being saved even then.

L. to r: the late Jack Bury, Arthur, Jack Wharton and members of the Stokes family, with the Fowler showman's engine number 1822, *King Edward.* The infant engine movement was not then strong enough to save it and it was cut up when boiler repairs were found to be necessary. From Arthur Napper's collection.

Although Frank Stephens and his staff had been a tower of strength to Arthur, they were, after all, a professional body with a salaried General Secretary. The original band of preservationists felt that an organisation of a more voluntary nature was needed, so in 1954 it was decided to form a club. It was to be called The National Traction Engine Club.

Steam at dawn for the 1953 Appleford Rally. The hallowed ground which saw the first race in 1950 is seen in the background. Photograph: courtesy of Alastair Dacre Lacy.

Arthur and the Burrell, *May Queen*, at the Witney Rally in 1953. Photograph: copyright Alan Martin, from Arthur Napper's collection.

To show just how helpful and efficient the Association had been, there follows a letter to an early enthusiast and the advertising poster for the 1954 rally, together with what must rank as one of the prototype entry forms. This last named, was to set a pattern which has stood the test of time and has yet to be bettered. It does, however, belie its age in one vital respect: nowhere is there any request for third party insurance and as for a boiler report, who worried about that sort of thing in those far-off, halcyon days?

The National Traction Engine and Tractor Association Incorporated.

(with which is Incorporated
The National Threshing Machine Owners Association
and The Steam Cultivation Development Association)

Telephone
Reading 60197
Established 1893

Telegrams
Threshaul Reading

Incorporated 1905

Duke Street Chambers,
1 & 3, Duke Street,
Reading,
Berkshire.

20th April, 1954.

Dear Sir,

    Thank you for your letter of 16th April.

    The nearest station to the Rally ground is Appleford Halt. Your Members should be sure to enquire whether the train on which they propose to travel is due to stop at Appleford Halt. If a party is to travel on the same train, the British Railways have offered to consider stopping trains at Appleford Halt which normally run through that station.

    I regret that the special admission tickets are not yet available, but I am making a note to send twelve of these as soon as they are ready. The nominal charge has been fixed at 1s.0d. in addition to the 1s.0d. payable for entry by way of Programme. I will also arrange to send to you twelve copies of the programme when these are printed.

          Yours faithfully,
THE NATIONAL TRACTION ENGINE AND
TRACTOR ASSOCIATION INCORPORATED

SECRETARY

For the benefit of Road Locomotive enthusiasts, it is
proposed to include in the Rally Programme a short history
of the vehicles entered in the various Events, and it
would be appreciated if a note on the vehicle outlining
its known history, could be given below:-

NOTES :

A Separate form should be used for each vehicle.

Completed entry forms should be returned not later
than the 17th April, 1954, to

The Secretary,
National Traction Engine and Tractor Association,
Duke Street Chambers, 1 and 3, Duke Street,
READING, Berks.,

from whom additional copies of the form may be obtained.

A reasonable quantity of coal, and water will be
supplied for competitors. A limited supply of coal may
be purchased at cost on the site for the return journey.

Vehicles must be on the Rally site by 11 a.m. on the
day of the Rally. Vehicles entered may be shedded on the
site before the day of the Rally, and may be left there
for a limited period after the Rally.

NATIONAL TRACTION ENGINE RALLY
to be held at
BRIDGE FARM, APPLEFORD, near Abingdon, Berkshire,
on
SATURDAY, 12th JUNE, 1954

E N T R Y   F O R M

Name of
Entrant ....

Address ....

Particulars of Vehicle Entered

Make ....Built ....
Date

N.H.P. .... Engine No. ....Number ....
Registration

Single or   Number of   How
Compound .... Shafts   ....Shod ....

Name of DRIVER ....

Name of MATE   ....

PLEASE MARK X IN SQUARE OPPOSITE EVENT(S)
FOR WHICH THIS VEHICLE IS ENTERED

C L A S S E S

ENGINE ELEGANCE:

1. STEAM TRACTORS   ☐

2. AGRICULTURAL TRACTION ENGINES   ☐

3. SHOWMEN'S ENGINES   ☐

RACES:

4. STEAM TRACTORS   ☐

5. STEAM TRACTORS (CHAIN-DRIVEN)   ☐

6. STEAM TRACTION ENGINES   ☐

7. SHOWMEN'S ENGINES   ☐

OBSTACLE COMPETITIONS:

8. STEAM TRACTORS   ☐

9. AGRICULTURAL TRACTION ENGINES   ☐

10. SHOWMEN'S ENGINES   ☐

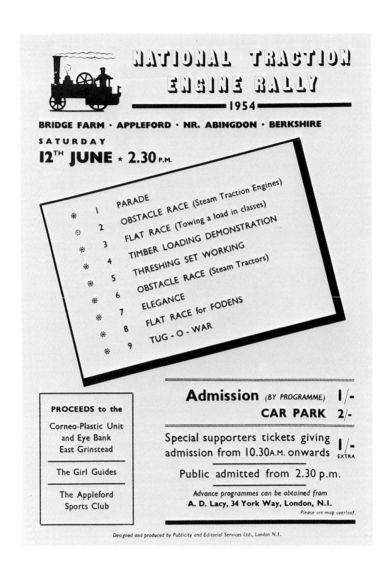

The poster that proclaimed Britain's first traction engine rally. Courtesy of Les Burberry.

The five contestants at the 1952 rally proceed to the scene of battle, led by Miles Chetwynd-Stapylton on the Aveling, *Ladygrove*. From Arthur Napper's collection.

In thoughtful mood at one of Britain's first traction engine events, on Sunday 8th June, 1952. Could Arthur perhaps be thinking, Whatever have I started? From the collection of Arthur Napper.

Chapter Five
Noggin and Natter

As in a lot of spheres, it turns out that in the field of holding traction engine rallies, the Americans beat us to it by at least three years. In 1951, reports came in of a massive Threshermen's Re-Union at Pontiac, Illinois, which went on for five days, "September 12 thru 16th", and all were invited to enjoy demonstrations of threshing, sawing, moving and setting, by no less that thirty-five engines! Added attractions included miniature engines and locomotives, steam cars, Jack North and his High School Orchestra, Bubbles Vaudeville, a square dance and an old fiddlers contest.

This was their third such gathering. The advertising promised that every moment would be filled with interesting activity for men and ladies. Provision was made for ample refreshment, safe drinking water and even free accommodation for those travelling from a distance. They obviously expected a very select clientele, as arrangements were made for landing facilities at Pontiac Airport for those coming by private 'plane! The general superintendent of this shindig was one Dan S. Zehr, who, with typical American enthusiasm, exhorted all to come and bring a car load and announced that he wished to meet everyone personally! One wonders how the harassed organisers of some of our larger rallies would cope with that!

Over here, Appleford and Nettlebed had done the trick nicely and enormous interest was being shown. What is not perhaps widely known, is that there was in fact a club, apart from The Road Locomotive Society, in existence in 1949. It was a purely local affair and centred round the preservation of two or three engines, the principal of which was the Burrell six n.h.p. showman's engine, number 3343 of 1911, *Princess Mary*. It was a laudable effort, but it wasn't to last, as attempts to preserve engines communally are nearly always doomed to failure. The great and lasting exception to this rule is The Gladiator Club in Cornwall, which for years has owned and operated the Burrell showman's engine of that name. One of the great bones of contention is always who is to be the engine driver and The Gladiator Club sensibly elected the most competent man they could find, the late 'Arch' Pethick. It is sad to relate that the last Burrell showman's engine of all, number 4092, *Simplicity*, ended up in the joint ownership of five people and a disagreement among them led to its destruction. The club of 1949 that I speak of, was based in the Thetford area and was headed by an ex-employee of Burrell's, Arthur Phoenix. He, and that most respected of steam historians, Ronald H. Clark, did, however, leave us one great legacy of their endeavours. It is the beautiful bronze memorial tablet on the wall of the old Burrell works in Minstergate Street, Thetford, depicting the enormous Burrell Boydell engine of 1856. Ronald Clark and Arthur Phoenix worked tirelessly to raise the money for its erection and it was unveiled with due ceremony in 1958. It can, of course, still be seen today.

Burrell showman's engine number 3925, *Princess Mary*, round which a club was formed in 1950, in the Thetford area of Norfolk. From the collection of Arthur Napper.

In perhaps one final attempt to survive in the post-steam era, The National Traction Engine Owners and Users Association decided in 1954 to modernise its image and change its name. It became The National Association of Agricultural Contractors, with premises in Bedford Row, London. Naturally enough, this change of identity did not suit the traction engine fraternity and it was decided to form The National Traction Engine Club. Seven interested people gathered at the home of Alastair Dacre Lacy at Shiplake in Berkshire, in May, 1954 and the Club was duly formed. Alastair Dacre Lacy was elected the first Chairman and the other founder members were Arthur Napper, Jack Wharton (current President of the N.T.E.C.), the late Frank

Upton, Giles Romanes, Frank Stephens and Donald Young.

The subscription was set at ten shillings and it was agreed to adopt the Appleford Rally as the main Club event and to publish a magazine. It was also agreed that members could attend the Rally free of charge, which was later to prove an unwise decision. Dacre Lacy's company designed the now famous red logo and the Club tie is based on the design of that worn by Old Etonians.

In the same way that it is amusing to look back on the rivalry between High and Low Church in the Church of England, it is also amusing to see how the august body of The Road Locomotive Society looked askance at the activities of the infant National Club. The Road Locomotive Society was, and still is, a learned society to which one had to be elected. A man who is a prominent member today had his application turned down flat with no reason given, even though he was a member of the Institute of Mechanical Engineers. He was also in the habit of driving a large road locomotive vast distances all over Britain.

Although nothing was ever put into print, not a few of the members seemed to view with horror the prospect of racing traction engines and, even worse, running them on the road. It seemed at one time that it was quite acceptable to photograph them, catalogue them and generally record them, the one thing that was frowned upon was to use them. The early newsletters record, in almost matter-of-fact tones, that so and so's fleet of engines had been sold to the local scrap merchant and was cut up on the spot. Amazingly, a list of makes, numbers, registration numbers, dates and names were then listed with scrupulous accuracy, but no attempt was made to urge the members to go out and buy the engines! Perhaps it should be remembered that in 1949 the membership total was only some twenty-five people, but it seems almost inconceivable that in those days an elitist attitude prevailed amongst some of the older professional steam engineers, who made up the bulk of the membership, and it has been intimated to me that some of them would almost have preferred to see 'their' engines cut up for scrap, rather than see them fall into the hands of, what they saw as, a bunch of dangerous amateurs and fanatics.

Today of course the two societies live very happily side by side and many people, including Arthur Napper and the author, are members of both. The Road Locomotive Society is still the foremost authority on the steam traction engine and its historical records, library and photographic collection are second to none. The National Club is very much more concerned with the running of a modern preservation movement, with the safety and legal aspects well to the fore. Insurance is another part of its work and publicity and contacting tourist boards yet another sphere of activity. Keeping the traction engine popular in the mind of the general public is important too, so a car sticker has just been brought out, which proclaims "I love traction engines"!

Frank Stephens, as General Secretary, got the Club off to a good start in 1954, incidentally combining a salaried position with the old N.T.E. and T. Association, with an honorary one with the new N.T.E.C., but various problems soon became apparent. The expense of not only running a rally, but also publishing a quality magazine was more than the meagre funds could stand. Although the early committee members were highly competent men in their own particular fields, and some of them fine steam engineers, they were in uncharted waters when it came to running a national amateur society, after all, nothing like it had ever been done before. As with a number of rallies since, not enough capital reserve was held against the risk of a wet weekend the following year. The 1956 Appleford Rally had been cancelled owing to a waterlogged field and the committee incurred quite heavy costs for advertising, printing and coal. This it could ill afford. Charitable generosity too had perhaps gone a little to their heads, as half the proceeds of the 1953 Appleford Rally had been set aside to send a twenty-five year old sailor to Switzerland, for an operation on one of his eyes. The little club couldn't sustain such largesse as well as a complete washout the following year and by January 1957 was all but bankrupt.

The accounts and paperwork were in chaos and Frank Stephens, already overworked, could not, by his own admission, give the Club's affairs the time they demanded. The Club had been presented with a Sentinel steam waggon by North Thames Gas and Stephens was instructed to write to them, asking permission to sell it, as there were nowhere near enough funds to contemplate restoring it. In fact, there were no funds at all.

Committee meetings had been held from the outset at the new offices of the N.A.A.C. at 52, Bedford Row, London. On the evening of the 21st August, a highly charged meeting was in progress. The Treasurer, Walter Edney, had heartbreaking news to impart. The Club was in the red to the tune of eighty-eight pounds. It must of course be remembered that this was 1957 and that today's equivalent would be at least ten times that amount. The position was indeed serious and there seemed to be no solution. Alan Martin was one who was there and he remembers proposing a motion, very reluctantly, that the Club be wound up. Arthur and his friends were completely poleaxed. All they had strived for and dreamed of was disintegrating, but facts had to be faced and debts had to be paid. Although the N.A.A.C. gave support in the form of 'lending' Frank Stephens as General Secretary, they were also not averse to charging the not inconsiderable sum of fifty pounds a year for the use of their offices for committee meetings.

As the Chairman, Ron Deamer, was absent, his place was taken by an ebullient and forceful Essex clergyman, the Revd. Philip Wright, who, of course, had had plenty of experience in raising funds for lost causes. He urged them all to put their thinking caps on and to try to come up with a solution.

All of a sudden, Arthur had a brainwave. It was a gamble that started it off in the first place, why not try a gamble to save it? He remembered that Arthur Phoenix had had a draw to raise funds for his Norfolk-based enterprise. "Why don't we hold a raffle?" he ventured. The committee threw back their heads and roared with laughter. "What for, a box of chocolates?" they chorused.

Then the Treasurer rose to his feet. "We shall indeed hold a raffle, not for a box of chocolates, but for an engine," he said. "And where, pray, do we get an engine from, out of a conjurer's hat?" sighed one disillusioned member. "I propose to present to the Club a ten ton steam-roller in working order, to be raffled during the coming nine months, the draw to take place at next year's Appleford Rally."

The committee, or most of them, were struck dumb. The minutes of the meeting make highly entertaining reading. Alan Martin, in the heat of the moment, looked a gift horse right in the mouth and said that he thought a traction engine would be a far greater incentive to the public to buy tickets! Arthur, quick to try and resolve the matter, said that he knew where there was a Garrett tractor on rubbers, in working order, which could be purchased for the sum of sixty pounds. The ensuing debate was, however, enough to change Edney's mind and his generosity that night seemed to know no bounds. He agreed to present the Club with a Wallis and Steevens traction engine that he owned, in place of the roller. He took out an overdraft of one hundred pounds on his own personal account, to tide the Club over and so that it could still function. He even agreed to pay the five pounds owed to all nineteen engine owners who had taken part in the washed-out 1957 Appleford event. Walter Edney had saved the Club.

Very valuable lessons had been learned and much experience gained. Charity begins at home was a wise maxim to be adopted for future years and the introduction of the first two-day rally meant that the profit was doubled, at the same initial expense.

Such was Walter Edney's enthusiasm for the movement, and his generosity, that earlier that same year when he had been so impressed with the maintenance of his 1910 Burrell, number 3201, and a teenage Michael Lugg's ability to drive it, he simply gave it to him.

It was Lugg's of Billingshurst who were despatched to Duncton Quarry to see if the Wallis that Walter Edney had presented to the Club was still steamable. It was duly found to be in working order and taken straight to Appleford.

The promoter and organiser of the raffle was John Crawley, the Vice-Chairman then; and now. As Editor of *Steaming*, the Club magazine, and as the organiser of more traction engine rallies than anyone, he is one of the 'greats' of the engine movement. He worked tirelessly promoting the sale of tickets and a teenage author can remember badgering relatives and friends to part with the not inconsiderable sum of five shillings.

MEMBERS ONLY

THE NATIONAL TRACTION ENGINE CLUB

N⁰ 2783

GRAND DRAW

STOKERIDGE, PRINTERS, BEDFORD

Prize : **A 7 n.h.p.**

Wallis & Steevens Expansion General Purpose **Traction Engine**

5/-

In good running order, which will be in steam at the Appleford Rally on 14th June, 1958, when the draw will take place. The winner is offered free parking at a number of different locations
Promoter : John Crawley, 51 Putnoe Lane, Bedford
This ticket acknowledges receipt of a donation of 5/- to the Club's funds. The prize will be given only to the member to whom the ticket was sold.

5/-

A draw ticket from the 1957 raffle that saved The National Traction Engine Club, won by a fourteen year old schoolboy. Courtesy of Colin Hawkins.

At the 1958 Appleford Rally, the grand draw took place and the winning ticket was number 7794. The Ranford family from Andover was enjoying a day out at the rally, but delight turned to consternation when the parents realised that their fourteen year old son, Christopher, had won the prize. By no stretch of the imagination was their front garden big enough to stable a traction engine. An amicable arrangement followed: the boy was given the sum of one hundred pounds and the engine was subsequently sold, the proceeds being added to Club funds.

Dr. Giles Romanes and Dr. Scott on an advertising stunt in Regent Street with *Eileen*. Fling Drinks apparently freshened and fortified in the early 'fifties. The local Chief Constable, however, was certainly not amused. Photograph: courtesy of Alastair Dacre Lacy.

From that day, The National Traction Engine Club has never looked back. Under the guiding hand of the Chairman, Anthony Heal, of the London department store of that name, and, latterly, Peter Barber, M.A., a consulting engineer, it has gone from strength to strength. Finances were looked after by Hamish Orr-Ewing, today Chairman of Jaguar, then latterly by Jack Hobbs, an accountant. On the committee for very many years, Arthur held the title of President between 1968 and 1971.

The Appleford Rally of 1971 was to be the last of over twenty highly enjoyable annual events. The reason for its demise was quite straightforward: it wasn't really needed, owing to a proliferation of events in the southern counties and the formation, during the 'sixties, of over forty-eight affiliated local clubs. With the rearrangement of land at Appleford, car parking had become something of a headache too.

Arthur Napper and Appleford were not, however, to be forgotten that easily. The little village was to be honoured with a steam spectacular every bit as memorable as the events of 1950. To celebrate the twenty-first anniversary of the founding of The National Traction

Engine Club and to pay a suitable tribute to Arthur, it was proposed to hold a road run from the old scene of battle at Nettlebed, back to Appleford. The organisation of such a venture was not possible without the co-operation of the Berkshire Constabulary. At first the Chief Constable was concerned about the amount of chaos it would cause, as nothing like it had ever been attempted before. Arthur recalls the final meeting with him. "Well," he said, "provided you keep out of Wallingford and go at two minute intervals, I suppose I shall have to let you have the road. One more thing," he added ominously, "this time round, if I catch any of you so and sos without the proper road tax, you're for the high jump." Arthur was delighted and the Club set about organising the event. The idea was novel, proved extremely popular and interest was shown from all over the country. The date fixed was Saturday July 12th, 1975. The scene on the field at Nettlebed on the previous evening was nothing if not impressive. No less than fifty-three engines, of all makes and descriptions, had arrived to do justice to the occasion.

Because of the risk of road congestion and delay, it was decided that the engines would indeed leave at two minute intervals, from eight a.m. First to set off on that memorable morning was a Sentinel steam waggon, owned by David Webster, representing The Shropshire Steam Engine Club. Being the fastest type of steam vehicle, two more Sentinels followed, one representing The Three Counties Society. Five Foden steam waggons, a Mann and a Yorkshire were next away. Looking as impressive as ever it did, Jack Wharton's Burrell showman's, *King George VI*, engaged top wheel and was soon lost to view. Next it was the turn of the nippy little five ton steam tractors. It fell to the little Garrett showman's tractor, *The Greyhound*, to represent the local Thames Valley Traction Engine Club, now in its twenty-fifth year. Societies and clubs were represented by engines from as far afield as Cornwall, Lancashire, Wales and Lincolnshire.

Giles Romanes was, fittingly, the last to leave that historic field aboard his little Wallis three ton tractor, *Goliath*. What a sight to behold and people in their thousands lined the route to watch.

The faster vehicles completed the run in about an hour, whereas the slower steamrollers took anything up to seven or eight hours to complete the course. It says a lot for the loving care bestowed upon these engines, that all fifty-three arrived in one piece and under their own steam. Of the twenty-four engines that had attended the first Club rally at Appleford in 1954, eight of them completed the 1975 run, a journey of almost twenty miles.

All the fun of the fair awaited the participants when they arrived, the entertainment, as always, was in the capable hands of the Hatwell Brothers, who had supported the Appleford Rally from the beginning and were the first of many travelling showmen to find that they had an affinity with the traction engine enthusiasts.

If the Chief Constable was quite happy with how it all went, then Arthur was simply over the moon. Here was proof, if proof was needed, that the traction engine had taken its rightful place in the affections of the British public. The movement had stood the test of time and that was really what they had come to celebrate; and celebrate they did! There was, after all, a very large beer tent and it would have been a shame not to have used it ... Everyone had a thoroughly enjoyable time and all the participants were presented with a memento of the occasion, in the form of a copy of the original licence that had got Giles Romanes into trouble at Nettlebed all those years before.

It was, however, on the Sunday evening, when it was all over and everyone was packing up and getting ready to go home, that something slightly untoward happened, or is alleged to have happened. Now, I am quite aware that some of my readers will believe in ghosts and that others most certainly will not. There was a man who worked for very many years for John Fowler and Company, whose name was Alf Pepper. He rose to quite a high position in the firm and his crowning achievement was to superintend the building and delivery of the very last Fowler showman's engine, number 20223, *Supreme*. In the last years of his life he took a tremendously keen interest in the restoration of this engine and, as a friend of the owner, Jack Wharton, was able to give much valuable information and help.

The incident occurred when *Supreme* had been loaded on to its low loader and the driver was just starting to move off. All of a sudden, three people in the crowd shouted to the driver to stop, as there was an old gentleman on the bed of the low loader. No sooner had the driver touched his brakes, than he was told to proceed. It is alleged that momentarily, the late Alf Pepper appeared.

As with all ghost stories, there is never any proof and the cynics will always explain it away by saying such things as it was a trick of the light, or too much to drink. The most important thing is that the three witnesses will all vouch for the fact that Alf Pepper was smiling.

Arthur (left), Peter Barker and Alfie Price, en route to an early Beaulieu Rally. Taken whilst stopped for water at King's Somborne. From Arthur Napper's collection.

The author at the age of fourteen steering for Arthur Napper on his Fowler single number 15710, *Tommy*, at the 1958 Andover Rally. From the author's collection.

A document that reads extraordinarily well and seemed to auger well for the future. On the contrary, it was not to last. Courtesy of Steve Neville.

The Steam Traction Engine Preservation Association

OWNERS, OPERATORS AND EXHIBITORS OF SHOWMAN, TRACTION & MODEL ENGINES

Hon. Secretary:
A. T. PHOENIX,
15-17, THE SQUARE, PIKE LANE,
THETFORD, NORFOLK.
Phone: 2114

An Appeal to Steam Engine Enthusiasts everywhere.

This Society, whose objects are to acquire, renovate, operate, exhibit and preserve Steam Traction Engines and other Historic Machinery, needs your financial and moral support.

You can help in many ways: by donations or Membership Subscriptions, by making connections and collections on our behalf, by donating or loaning equipment, photographs and negatives, by helping us to clean and re-paint our Burrell Showman "Princess Mary" and other Engines in our possession.

We need a dynamo, belting, cable, lamps, side curtains for the "Princess" and anything else thats useful for any of our Engines.

You can also help by writing to the Press in support of our undertaking and proposal to stage an Exhibition of Steam Traction and Model Engines at Thetford during the Festival of Britain, and by recommending our Association to your friends.

We need under cover accommodation, and the support of Local Authorities to help us stage our Exhibitions in Thetford and elsewhere.

Our Thetford Exhibition is intended to Commemorate the Achievements of all Manufacturers of Steam Road Engines and Charles Burrell & Sons of Thetford in particular.

We actually operate Steam Traction Engines, and our Engines and Models are open to inspection by appointment to genuine inquirers.

Our project has the approval of Parry Billings, Esq., Local Government Liason Officer for the Festival of Britain; and the support of Geoffrey D. M. Block, M.A., and Ronald H. Clark, M.I.M.E., the author of "Steam Engine Manufacturers of Norfolk," and of "Suffolk, Essex and Cambridgeshire."

It is hoped that Ronald Clark's New Book, "The History of Burrells" will be on sale during the Exhibition.

We have gone to considerable expense in collecting Engines and Models for Exhibition, our funds are not unlimited, and the time has arrived when others should be invited to lighten our financial burden.

Offers of other Engines, Models, and Historic Machinery are invited.

Will **YOU** help?

72

An amusing glance at the committee of the 1955 Appleford Rally, commissioned by Alastair Dacre Lacy and featuring a youthful Arthur Napper. Cartoon by Alan Course, reproduced by courtesy of Alastair Dacre Lacy.

Chapter Six
Arthur in the Bar

"Did you know," said Arthur to me one evening, "that Wilson's went from steam to diesel and back to steam again?" The quick answer to that was that I didn't and it serves to show the vast extent of Arthur's knowledge on the subject.

To meet Arthur Napper for the first time can be a slightly unnerving experience. One somehow expects to meet a tall man, very brash, with plenty to boast about. The man one in fact meets is small in stature, very quietly spoken, with the softest of Berkshire accents and no pretensions whatsoever. He has a sense of humour second to none and absolutely revels in the foibles and slight eccentricities of his fellows. Being a natural mimic, he can, of course, turn his Berkshire accent on and off at will, with devastating effect upon those at whom his humour is directed. Although he is never malicious, beware one thing: Arthur has a knack of spotting humbug and pomposity at twenty paces. Woe betide the man who tries to make out that he knows more than Arthur does, or that he has done more than he has. On such occasions, Arthur has been known to explode in a highly spectacular fashion, leaving the recipient of his wrath feeling less than inches tall. He harbours no bad feelings and all that remains is just another hilarious story, to be related in his inimitable style at the next meeting he attends. His real fury, however, is reserved for the increasingly stupid antics of the motorists he comes across whilst driving an engine. The author has had the pleasure of being Arthur's assistant during the writing of this book and can vouch for the fact that his comments are invariably highly original, but also quite unprintable! He was known on one occasion to lob a lump of coal in the direction of one fellow traveller, who he considered to be hellbent on committing suicide!

"Did you know that there was a race before mine?" he asked another time. Well apparently there was and it involved six Aveling and Porter steamrollers, which were making Barton Stacey Army Camp before the War. Being a military installation, only the Irish navvies took part and they raced for quite high stakes. They also lost quite a lot of money!

Only once did the bookies turn up at a traction engine rally. That was at Appleford in 1954 and they placed sizeable odds on Arthur winning, but it was a once-only occasion.

Lifting the tar for two miles on the Newbury to Andover road with his

Fowler, *Tommy*, one hot summer's day, caused Arthur a bit of a headache. "I shouldn't worry about it" said Jack Lawrence, his life-long friend and assistant, when they had pulled off the road. "You shouldn't worry" replied Arthur, somewhat vexed, "it'll be me the Road Surveyor will be after when he discovers half his bloody main road missing and what's more, he won't have far to go for it when he sees most of it wrapped round our back wheels!"

Judging by the blurred strakes, Arthur and his steersman, Jack Lawrence, are driving *Tommy* along at a cracking pace, on their way home from the Andover Rally, on 15th May, 1960. This engine is still owned by Arthur and is Fowler single number 15710, built in 1920. Photograph: copyright J.W. Peirson, from the collection of Arthur Napper.

To say that Arthur is a fine engineman is the understatement of the year. Quite simply, he never misses a trick, or, by his own admission, he only did so once. He was returning from a charity fête at Shottesbrooke Park, steering for Alfie Price on the latter's five ton Burrell tractor. The steersman's seat had come adrift and Arthur tried to readjust it. Momentarily he took his eyes off the road. A second later the front wheel hit the verge and the engine all but disappeared into the hedge. It required a crane to get the engine out. At first sight, Arthur's injuries appeared to be serious and he was rushed to Maidenhead Hospital.

Better news followed and he was allowed home on the proviso that he had a nice cup of tea. He recalls tipping the tea down the sink and pouring himself a large whisky instead!

The only time Arthur ever missed a trick, resulting in hospital treatment for him and a crane to recover Mr. A. Price's little Burrell five ton tractor. Happily, no lasting damage was done to either Arthur or the engine. From Arthur Napper's collection.

Only once, again by his own admission, was he ever foolhardy. He took on a steersman's challenge, that however fast Arthur got the engine to go, he could steer it. As we've seen, always a man for a challenge, Arthur pressed the old Wantage along at nearly full regulator and seeing that the road was pretty straight, the steersman kept his side of the bet. When they came to the sharp right-hand bend at Long Wittenham, however, his luck ran out. The engine veered to the wrong side of the road and the head-on collision with an oncoming lorry was inevitable. "You stupid mad fools," yelled the lorry driver, surveying the wrecked vehicle that was perched crazily on the front wheel of the engine. "You just wait 'til I get out of this jam, " he went on, "I'm going straight into Wallingford to fetch the Police." "Yes and one more puff from this engine," said Arthur quietly, "and you will be backside over tip and on your side in the ditch, then you won't be going anywhere."

Contract timber hauling and land clearance were jobs that came Arthur's way until relatively recently and he always enjoyed the work. Once, as a subcontractor in 1938, he was clearing land in Abingdon when a dispute arose as to whether the work could proceed. The local Police were called and they ordered the work to stop. Since Arthur and Tommy Yeo were on piecework and had received no instructions from the main contractor, they decided to keep working. "Stop operations at once," boomed the Sergeant, "you are not to pull out one single tree more." Arthur noticed that the wire rope from the engine was lying in the grass between the policeman's legs. "Is that your last word?" enquired Arthur. "Indeed it is, I am rooted to the spot," snapped the Sergeant in reply. With that, Arthur gently opened the regulator ...

Before an admiring crowd of onlookers, Arthur unloads his Fowler, *Tommy*, named after his great friend and teacher, the late Tommy Yeo. From Arthur Napper's collection.

He has appeared regularly on television and has been interviewed on a number of occasions, both for local radio and for newspaper and magazine articles. At the Windsor Show he was presented to Prince Philip, who held a lively discussion with him on the single engine ploughing system that he could remember working on Romney Marsh. He is a founder member of The Thames Valley Traction Engine Club and, in this, its twenty-fifth year, he has been elected President for life, an honour which he much cherishes.

Arthur has won countless awards and trophies over the years. Here he receives one of The National Traction Engine Club's highest awards, The Golden Film Trophy, from Anthony Mellor, the then Editor of the *World's Fair*, in October 1964. Photograph: copyright B.J. Finch, from Arthur Napper's collection.

Today, Arthur lives in semi-retirement in a delightful riverside house, just over the railway from Bridge Farm. From the picture window of his elegant drawing room, one's eye is drawn across the meadow to his engine house, where the smokeboxes of his beloved engines, *Old Timer*, *Tommy* and the new girl, *Dorothy*, can just be seen. He still farms land at East Hagbourne, with dairy and arable interests, but his absorbing occupation today is the breeding of beautiful golden Tamworth pigs. He and his partner in the venture, Mrs. Kathleen Pile, have been so successful, that Mrs. Pile was awarded third prize at the 1985 Royal Show at Stoneleigh.

Old Timer and *Tommy* are in semi-retirement too, as they are still on steel wheels, but they always emerge for the President's Steam Party, which Arthur hosts every autumn.

His latest acquisition is the Burrell road locomotive number 4093, *Dorothy*, which glides him in almost uncanny silence to the local rallies, where he is, of course, a celebrity.

Burrell number 4093, *Dorothy*, Arthur's latest acquisition, which glides him in almost uncanny silence to the local rallies. It was the penultimate Burrell to be built and was completed by Garrett's of Leiston in 1931. From Arthur Napper's collection.

On reflection, he is pleased to remember how it all started and simply amazed at how it has grown into a way of life for some and an absorbing hobby for so many more. He will go to the most extraordinary lengths to help a fellow engine owner and is glad to see how so many youngsters are taking steam to their hearts. "Without them," he says, "it could all die out again."

A steam engine is not the sort of thing that one stores anywhere and many owners have been grateful to Arthur for storage facilities at Bridge Farm. One such was Ran Hawthorne, for many years Editor of the Club journal, *Steaming*. He stored his Fowler steamroller with Arthur and on one occasion asked him if he was quite sure it wasn't in the way. "Of course it isn't" replied Arthur, "your engine is the first thing I see when I look out in the morning and the sight of it starts my day off just fine."

Burrell number 4093, *Dorothy*, when brand new in 1931. From the collection of Arthur Napper.

The words modest and legend, are not ones that Arthur would readily apply to himself. On holiday last year in Devon, however, he came across a steamroller on its way to a rally, stuck in a lay-by. He stopped and suggested to the driver that if he were to put both driving pins in and put him in top gear (he invariably refers to engines as he), the roller would move.

The driver could think of no better solution to his predicament and did as Arthur suggested. With a few sharp barks from the chimney, the roller was free. "Thanks very very much" said the young roller driver. "By the way, where do you come from?" "I come from Berkshire" replied Arthur. "Oh, good heavens," grinned the roller driver, "you must be one of the Arthur Napper brigade!" "Well," said Arthur, "I have met him on a couple of occasions." With that, he got into his car and drove away.

Another of Arthur's engines. This cut down Foden waggon was capable of very high speeds and was, for a short time, owned by the author. From the collection of Arthur Napper.

Old Timer must have led more grand parades than any other engine in preservation. From the collection of Arthur Napper.

The crowd is jubilant as Arthur romps home, the winner of yet another race, at Northleach, in July 1958. Photograph: copyright Alan Martin, from the collection of Arthur Napper.

Fowler showman's, *King Edward*, raising steam to take part in the 1954 Appleford Rally, which was, sadly, to be her last. Photograph: copyright Alan Martin, from Arthur Napper's collection.

Such was Arthur's enthusiasm that even the girls pitched in to clean *Old Timer*, under the direction of Arthur's sister, Maureen (top left). Photograph: Cole, from Arthur Napper's collection.

Arthur Napper (left) with the author on the footplate of *Old Timer*.
Photograph: Michael Rice.

Those who have read his book, *A Little and Often*, will know that Chris Edmonds has been devoted to steam traction engines all his life. One person who he met when pursuing his quest to purchase his first engine was none other than the subject of this book himself, Arthur Napper. Arthur's sheer enthusiasm in the early 'fifties in the cause of the traction engine has been an inspiration to countless thousands, including the author.

Being a personal friend of Arthur, it has long been one of Chris' ambitions to chronicle, in detail, the events of those early years and his research has resulted in an almost incredible story.

Chris Edmonds was born in 1944 and is today in business on his own account. For the past fifteen years he has been Organist and Director of Music at St. Mark's Church, High Wycombe. Although at present no longer an engine owner, he still keeps his hand in as assistant driver, or steersman, to some of his many friends, including this year, to his great delight, Arthur Napper.